Tragic Beauty

The Dark Side of Venus Aphrodite and the Loss and Regeneration of Soul

Tragic Beauty

The Dark Side of Venus Aphrodite and the Loss and Regeneration of Soul

Arlene Diane Landau

CHIRON PUBLICATIONS • ASHEVILLE, NORTH CAROLINA

© 2019 by Chiron Publications. All rights reserved. No part of this publication may be reproduced, stored in a retrieval system, or transmitted, in any form by any means, electronic, mechanical, photocopying, recording, or otherwise, without the prior written permission of the publisher, Chiron Publications, P.O. Box 19690, Asheville, N.C. 28815-1690.

www.ChironPublications.com

Previously published by Spring Journal Books

Cover Art: Edvard Munch, "Modonna," 1894-95 © 2011 The Munch Museum / The Munch-Ellingsen Group / Artists Rights Society (ARS), NY.

Image Source: Madonna, 1894-95 (oil on canvas) by Edvard Munch (1863-1944) National Museum, Oslo, Norway/ The Bridgeman Art Library

Cover design and typography by Northern Graphic Design & Publishing

Backcover Author Photograph: Philip Westgren

Printed primarily in the United States of America.

ISBN 978-1-63051-776-2 paperback
ISBN 978-1-63051-777-9 hardcover
ISBN 978-1-63051-778-6 electronic
ISBN 978-1-63051-779-3 limited edition paperback

Library of Congress Cataloging-in-Publication Data Pending

Contents

Dedication

For Alexis and Brad

Acknowledgments

I wish to express my deep gratitude to Nancy Cater of Spring Journal Books for her enthusiastic acceptance and support in the publication of this book, and to my editor, Sylvia Ruud, for her diligence and patient assistance in weaving the loose ends of my original manuscript together into so whole a fabric. I also wish to thank Margaret Ryan, who has edited my work for so many years, for her support and friendship.

My appreciation extends to my Jungian colleagues, Lyn Cowan, Linda Schierse Leonard, Nancy Qualls-Corbett, and Stanton Marlan for their support and thoughtful characterizations of the present writing. Here I also sincerely thank those patients who have granted me permission to include their dreams and without whom this book may not have come to be.

To my sweet girlfriends, Jeanie Patterson, Mary von Aspe, and Peggy Miller, with whom I have been fortunate to remain so close and share so many stories about the Goddess through more years than I dare say, I convey my continual love and gratitude.

I also thank my beloved and knowledgeable daughter, Alexis Landau Westgren, and my creative and resourceful husband and colleague, Brad TePaske, for their support and sensitivity to me through the years of my researching the text and in the many discussions we have shared concerning it. Their love and confidence in me as well as the support they have brought to this project and my life will always remain essentially incalculable. To Philip Westgren, and Marcus and Jonas TePaske, I also convey many thanks for the love and liveliness that you bring to my life.

Finally, I express my gratefulness to the Jungian analysts and supervisors with whom I have worked over the years, some since passed from this earth. And to the grace of God that led me to C.G. Jung and allowed me take in and digest and understand the eternal waters of life.

Foreword

Aphrodite women always stand out. Go to any public venue and wait for the moment of recognition: *There she is*—the "it" girl. Tall and slim, or short and slim, blond or raven or red-haired, it matters not. Whether she dresses like a princess or a prostitute, she has the unmistakable spark that is the touch of Aphrodite.

Aphrodite is the golden goddess of love and beauty in Greek mythology. Women who embody the Aphrodite archetype have much less choice in how they behave or react than they, or others, imagine. The myths tell us that Aphrodite qualities are essential for the joy of life, but the shadow side of Aphrodite manifests when a woman is completely identified with Aphrodite's powers, when other archetypal qualities of the feminine are unimportant to her. The tragedies that result from this are the subject of numerous well-known novels and films and exemplified in the lives of certain actresses and other celebrities, all considered here.

The dark side of the pursuit of beauty is especially apparent with aging, when the Aphrodite woman must become something other than a source of beauty or dwindle to a bitter and lonely end. Those whose lives have been wounded by the shadow side of Aphrodite—or those who do not have enough of Aphrodite's joy in their personal makeup—may find understanding and rebirth through the consciousness gained in this real-life exploration of an ideal that has ballooned into a distortion. In these times, when the idolization of Aphrodite—and the tragedy that ensues—are perhaps more widespread than ever, the crucial key for women is *consciousness*.

Chapter 1

Who Is Aphrodite?

Muse, tell me the deeds of golden Aphrodite...[1]

—Hesiod

These reflections on Aphrodite (whom the Romans called Venus) trace the unfolding of a personal, a mythological, and a depth-psychological realization that was always patiently waiting to dawn upon me. As a girl, I simply grew up doing these things, acting this way, not knowing that something alive from ancient times—a ubiquitous archetypal pattern, animate and breathing—was causing chaos by doing its own autonomous thing in my girl psyche. The *Third Homeric Hymn to Aphrodite* might well have described me in saying, "That seductive face of hers is always smiling, always carrying its seductive flower."[2]

Aphrodite girls *always* stand out. As James Hillman says, "Psyche serves in the temple of Aphrodite. Aphrodite is what makes something light up so you want it. She's the touch of beauty."[3] I recently experienced this "touch of beauty" while walking around in the Old Town of Prague. I noticed some commotion in the street. Then I saw "her" and her less fascinating entourage. She was magnificent. Of indeterminate race or ethnic group, she was olive-skinned, blue-eyed, and had long hair styled in many braids. Dressed in very short shorts and a tiny top, she was tall and thin, with high, strappy heels that glided easily over the nearly unwalkable cobblestone streets. Her companions were also scantily dressed, but their appearance scarcely had the same impact. When one sees a real incarnation of "her," one knows it. There is an aphroditic "vibe" that takes over; this woman's entourage of male and female "acolytes" knew she was the queen and that she must be served. When in full regalia, such women carry a divine spark. The other girls or women may be just as pretty, if one really looks at them, and "she" might even be less beautiful—but she is still the "it" girl.

Several years ago, I was in the Gallery Lafayette in Berlin, on the third floor in the hip, younger section. There she was again. She was tall and slim, with long black hair slicked back in a tight, high ponytail. She wore a short-cropped, white rabbit jacket in a baseball style and an electric blue top under the fluffy jacket, with matching electric blue, pointed stiletto heels. She wore very tight, white stretch jeans. She carried a very small purse encrusted with fake stones. She was introverted and private. I watched her every move, knowing that she was the one—one of the species. There are not so many of them in Berlin as in Beverly Hills or Manhattan. She finally made her purchase, which was a metallic belt studded with colorful stones. She was already wearing a similar belt studded with clear rhinestones. She walked out of the department and down the escalator, and all the male department store workers had their eyes on her. This was unusual since in Berlin, unlike Los Angeles, people do not exchange much eye contact, nor do they stare. The original Aphrodite, of course, had her golden girdle, which she loaned to Hera to attract Zeus. I am sure that this lovely daughter of Aphrodite did not know the ancient story, but she was, without doubt, an Aphrodite woman from birth. She did not appear to be an abused type, or slutty, but just Aphrodite pure and simple.

A twenty-one-year-old girl I know, named Jeannie, was living in Lisbon, Portugal. A boy who was in love with her—but about whom she was ambivalent—flew to Lisbon to be with her. Jeannie met up with this young man, and in high, stiletto heels, she walked with him on the streets of Lisbon for ten hours. I asked Jeannie how she could bear being in four-inch stilettos for so many hours on the uneven paths of the city. She said, "Aphrodite, who is my patron saint, helped me out." With the help of Aphrodite, her legs did not tire and her feet were not in pain—it is as though another force lifted her along the way. Aphrodite types are not into comfort when they wish to allure.

The other day I saw an old, tragic Aphrodite, bent over, walking— or barely walking—down Wilshire Boulevard in Santa Monica, California. She was about ninety years old, thin, dressed in tight pants and a low-cut leopard-print blouse, her hair piled up into an ancient "beehive." She was wearing pumps that were so high and pointed she could hardly walk. In her hands were high-heeled boots with fur trim on top that she was taking to the shoemaker; I watched her totter into his shop.

I know of a recent widower who was eighty-five and fell head over heels in love with an "ingénue" of seventy-five. She was all whispers, smiles, and girlishness, not "dried up" at all. This grandfather's son and daughter could not understand what had happened to their father, but one look at this seventy-five-year-old "ingénue," and I could see the power moving through her, attracting this rich old man who wanted to marry her after knowing her for only a couple of days.

Aphrodite women are not the ones who are bridesmaids but never a bride—they have many marriage proposals and engagements, often until they are quite old. No other goddess shines like she does at a party. Extraverted or introverted, she will plan her outfit—the right outfit—for days in advance. She is in her element. She will often single out a man, and you will see the two of them, as the evening progresses, on a couch in a room away from the group, in deep conversation. She will know just how to ask him about his work and interests, and he will respond—enchantment is her tool.

The quick glance works well for Aphrodite, too—she is the one who knows to lower her eyes, to stand a certain way. She is the one to attract a man across a crowded room. She knows she is the one that an available man will approach. She glances, and before long he returns the glance. She only has to stand there quietly with her wineglass in her hand; he will come over to her. It is sometimes painful for her sisters, her girlfriends, to witness this and not feel forlorn, ugly, and abandoned. I know a thirty-five-year-old woman who asked an Aphrodite woman in her sixties to go to a bar with her—the thirty-five-year-old knew that this much older woman could attract men, and hopefully the younger woman would then meet someone, too—the older woman would work as her bait. Aphrodite can speak volumes with one glance.

APHRODITE'S ORIGINS

Aphrodite is the golden goddess of love and beauty in Greek mythology. The Roman goddess Venus closely resembles her. The

Greeks believed that Aphrodite had a dual nature. As Aphrodite of All the People, she is the patroness of physical love. As Aphrodite Urania (Aphrodite of the Sky), she inspires spiritual and intellectual love. Eros, the god of love, is her companion and, according to some myths, her son. Eros stimulates autonomous desire by shooting his victims with arrows.

Aphrodite married Hephaestus, the lame and deformed blacksmith of the gods. She had love affairs with Ares, the god of war, and with Anchises, a Trojan prince. Aphrodite also loved Adonis, a handsome young hunter. When a wild boar killed Adonis, Aphrodite begged Zeus to restore him to her. The Greeks also worshiped Aphrodite as a goddess of fertility who created and sustained life. Greenness is equated with the vegetation spirit belonging to the life principle of Aphrodite.

In the *Iliad*, Aphrodite is the daughter of Zeus, but in later poems she is said to have sprung from the foam of the sea. Her name means "the foam-risen" (the Greek word *aphros* means sea-foam). In Hesiod, she is born from the severed testicles and foam of the sea after Kronos has castrated his father. The *Homeric Hymn* says that without her, there is no joy or Eros in the world. When Aphrodite is present there is movement and change. She is the goddess of "loveliness and desirability, graces with which you overwhelm mortal men, and all the immortals."[4] To her sphere of influence Hesiod assigns "girlish dalliance, smiles, deceits; sweet pleasure, love, and gentleness."[5] Among the early lyric poets she came to stand for a cultural ideal: the life devoted to youthful beauty and love. Aphrodite was the archetype of female beauty and love.

The Greek Aphrodite is only one of the many love goddesses of world mythology who personify these traits and qualities. Aphrodite's Roman sister, Venus, is one example, as is the Hindu Parvati, and other divine images. These mythological figures are all culturally distinct representations of a universal, transpersonal *archetype* at work. The archetype is a fundamental concept in the work of C.G. Jung. In his usage of the term, archetypes are those deepest premises of psychic functioning that delineate how we perceive and relate to the world. They are primordial structures in the human psyche that come from the collective unconscious and are the source of all myths, fairy tales, and religions. Jung states that the archetype "makes itself felt in the numinosity and fascinating power of the archetypal image."[6] Women who embody Aphrodite are themselves in the grip of her "numinosity and fascinating power."

I encountered an example of this fascinating archetypal power in a halfway house where I worked years ago with highly disturbed patients. There was one woman who had captured the hearts of all the male patients. They wanted to marry her; for them she embodied the image of desire. I was interested in meeting her and expected that she would be outwardly very beautiful. However, I was amazed to observe that she was dumpy and had no attribute that could be equated with any collective notion of beauty. Nevertheless, Aphrodite seemed to be channeled through her being without her conscious participation. I could feel her pull, and it was seductive for me as well as for the men and women in the halfway house who had fallen under her spell. It was hard for me not to become tangled up in her story and her web. I felt I wanted to be around her and close to her essence, her "smell." Joyce Carol Oates describes this particular species of feminine sexuality in a darkly lurid way:

> At first glance you would think that she was beautiful, glamorous—but no, she was neither beautiful nor glamorous so much as a mockery of "feminine" beauty, glamour—a cosmetic mask that has been disfigured. Her face was large, round, moon-shaped like my mother's, but it appeared to be shiny as if rubbed with a greasy rag, and swollen. Her shoulder-length hair was a dyed-beet color that looked frizzy and matted as if she'd just gotten out of bed. Over her ample body she was wearing something lacy and black and slinky—a nightgown? "negligee"? —and over this a man's flannel shirt carelessly buttoned so that you could see, without wishing to see, a swath of black lace and large, heavy lard-colored breasts. Like her face the woman's body appeared swollen, goitrous. Yet she exuded a weird sexual assurance with an elaborately painted crimson mouth, plucked and pencil-thin eyebrows, doll-like features squashed together inside the fatty face. There was a woman—a female—whose attraction for men would be powerful, I thought. Like certain of the older and more mature high school girls whom I knew, she seemed to belong to another species of being.[7]

Andrew Samuels writes: "Archetypes arouse affect, blind one to realities and take possession of will. To live archetypally is to live without limitations (inflation)."[8] Attempting to live without limitations inevitably leads to tragedy. Tragic figures in literature who are identified with Aphrodite include Tolstoy's Anna Karenina, Nastasya in *The Idiot* by Dostoevsky, and Flaubert's Madame Bovary. These three women, because of their almost complete identification with Aphrodite, suffered greatly and were destroyed by the love that drove and possessed them. Their fate calls to mind a contemporary example of a psychologist I know, whose repressed or unlived Aphrodite nature came to the surface when she fell into the depths of despair after falling in love with a patient. She experienced abandonment and heartbreak in the autonomous erotic disaster that ensued. In Johnny Cash's words, "Love is a burning thing / And it makes a fiery ring / Bound by wild desire / I fell into a ring of fire."[9]

Edward Edinger tells us that involvement with Aphrodite can lead one toward disaster—however, to ignore her can also be perilous.[10] In one Greek myth, Hippolytus, the son of the hero Theseus, values chastity above all and refuses the call of love. In retaliation for this slight, Aphrodite casts a spell over his stepmother Phaedra, causing her to fall passionately in love with him. Phaedra makes advances to him and then, when he rejects her, she goes to Theseus and lodges a charge of rape by Hippolytus. Theseus calls upon Poseidon to destroy his son and, in answer, a bull comes out of the sea as Hippolytus is riding in his chariot along the coast, and his horses bolt as he is dragged to his death.

Aphrodite's associations with the grave—her "dark shadow" and her connection to death—are not as well known as her many other attributes. Karl Kerenyi refers to these dark aspects as her "nocturnal connections," which have "more to do with a 'night of death' rather than a 'night of love.'"[11] During the first and second centuries, in Delphi, the Greeks worshiped Aphrodite as *Epitymbidia*, which means, "she upon the graves." Other epithets for her have included Aphrodite "killer of men," Aphrodite the unholy, and Aphrodite "the grave robber." Kerenyi summarizes: "All of these characteristics are evidence that at one time there were tales which identified the goddess of love with the goddess of death."[12]

The ideal of beauty often obscures the dark, death-like side of Aphrodite. Nonetheless, it is all around us. It is ubiquitous in literature and film, and I see it in the stories and dreams of my patients (and, of course, in my own life).

A poignant example of the dark side of the pursuit of beauty is that of an Aphrodite-like, sometime-prostitute patient who is an actress. Although not overweight, she chose to undergo a second tummy tuck and came close to death from infection; pus leaked from her artificially flat abdomen. Despite the experience of this life-threatening procedure, she decided to have surgery for a third time because she did not like the scars. She also had her breasts implanted a number of times.

When I worked in films, twenty-five years ago, to my astonishment I learned that breast implants were very common, as one actress friend after another took me to a dark corner of the musty set to show me the scars underneath her breasts. The practice of breast enlargement began in post-World War II Japan, when young Japanese women had industrial-strength transformer coolant injected into their breasts to meet the breast-size standards of American GIs. Another surge in the practice occurred in the 1960s, when topless showgirls in Las Vegas had liquid silicone pumped into their breasts.

Prostitution is common among women who identify with Aphrodite. The cult of Aphrodite, after all, numbered prostitutes among its followers. Indeed, in antiquity, sandals similar to what contemporary daughters of Aphrodite might wear were displayed as a logo at the door of a house of prostitution. From ancient traditions in the Near East to the temple cult of Corinth in Greece, ritual prostitution was considered sacred; indeed, the priestesses of the cult of Ishtar were also prostitutes. In the Bible, we have a picture of Jezebel who "painted her eyes and dressed her hair."

The young man mentioned above, who walked in Lisbon with Jeannie, began to write her long letters and then flew back to Lisbon again and began to stalk her. The police were eventually called in to examine the letters for any real threat to Jeannie. This young man may have a permanent police record due to Aphrodite's troublesome side. He became somewhat psychotic during the height of his so-called love—which could also be described as the possession of his psyche by Aphrodite. This is an example of the destruction that can be engendered when someone is in the grip of Aphrodite. Such things happened a number of times to this girl who kept alluring men— Aphrodite can't stick and can't say no.

This brings to mind an Aphrodite-identified friend who felt shamed that her new boyfriend was a plumber. This occupation did not mesh with this particularly wealthy but older Aphrodite's idea of who she should be with—she felt she should be with the high and mighty, but they were no longer interested in an aging woman. This woman gave her plumber much pleasure when she first met him— and then so much grief when she abandoned him without any feeling when the next "one" came. She told me many times that she would not be with anyone who would not continually treat her with the best of things—five-star hotels and the first-class section in airplanes on her many trips. Aphrodite has now punished her, perhaps for her imitation of love without any real love or care for others. She has ended up with a man who is very poor, who does not own a car, and is a fitness instructor to elderly women—which is how my friend met him. She is now jealous of the women he teaches to lift weights, and she has to pay for everything; on trips, they fly coach!

Another tale of Aphrodite's dark power is that of a woman whose husband was in the throes of a stroke—yet she could not resist flirting with the ambulance driver. Her behavior is an example of how hot Aphrodite can be such a cold, inhuman bitch. As William Faulkner observed, "The ungirdled mind is anyone's to take."[13]

For an Aphrodite woman, Eros's arrow can pierce at any time. If one is made of the stuff of the goddess of love, one may have no choice but to obey Aphrodite. Such a woman has much less choice in how she behaves or reacts than she—or others—imagine. The more archetypally identified our nature, the less our sense of choice. We are then pulled by fate.

John Sanford explains that "to meet our fate with courage requires from us character; character in Greek means a stamp or imprint."[14] Thus to have character, one must have some definition, some mark of individuality. Undifferentiated Aphrodites think that they are stunningly individual, but in terms of character, they are the opposite—they are highly collective. Flaubert's *Madame Bovary* comes to mind. Flaubert took a commonplace story of adultery and made of it a novel that has continued to be read because of its profound humanity and its archetypal underpinning. Emma Bovary considers herself to be special, but she is actually a bored, predictable, and unhappy middle-class wife whose general dissatisfaction with life leads her to act out her romantic fantasies and embark on an ultimately disastrous love affair. She destroys her life by embracing passion from an unconscious pedestal of inflation. She steadfastly ignores material reality, and is relentlessly drawn to financial ruin and suicide. Sanford explains that the more one identifies with an archetype, the more inflated one becomes, and the more special one feels, the farther one falls.

Today we see a different type of Aphrodite on Rodeo Drive than when I was young. We see beautiful young women, their long, chemically straightened blond hair hanging down their backs; their uniform breasts and thin, muscular bodies. Underneath their jeans and thongs are perfectly groomed vulvas, but if one looks carefully at their arms one might see the needle marks of heroine addiction, or if one looks behind their ears one might see the stitches of the cosmetic surgeon. A woman who from a distance looks thirty might really be fifty. Often these women are yearning and hurt little girls, with little core inside and no place to go outside. I saw one such woman in Beverly Hills the other day. She was finishing an early dinner with her husband and two young Britney-Spears-look-alike daughters—they had long blond hair, huge bell bottoms, and tiny tank tops. Their mother, in her late thirties, was beautiful and had long blond hair, a very short skirt, huge breasts—and, trailing behind her, innocent and out-of-it looking, her husband in his doctor scrubs: obviously a Beverly Hills surgeon. I detected her anger at her life—but little did she know that she was in thrall to an ancient goddess and losing the chance to live an individual life.

APHRODITE: JOY AND SHADOW

The myths and ancient hymns tell us that Aphrodite qualities are essential for the joy of life, but the shadow side of Aphrodite manifests when the archetype has consumed a woman, when she is completely identified with Aphrodite's powers, when other archetypal qualities of the feminine are unimportant to her. The tragedies that result from this are the subject of numerous well-known novels and films, as we shall see in chapter 2, and exemplified in the lives of certain actresses and other celebrities, which we consider in chapter 3.

Where do we look to find those feminine qualities that might balance Aphrodite's excesses? The natural place to look is where

Aphrodite herself was first named—in the myths and legends of ancient Greece and Rome. And here we find Aphrodite's sisters, goddesses who have very different approaches to feminine being. In chapter 4 we will meet some of them and consider their importance in balancing Aphrodite in the psyche of an individual woman.

Those whose lives have been wounded by the shadow side of Aphrodite—or, on the other hand, those who do not have enough of Aphrodite's joy in their personal makeup—may find understanding and rebirth through the consciousness gained in analysis or therapy. In chapters 5 and 6, we look at what the process of such therapy may be, how dreams may contribute to this, and the clarification provided by the psychology of C.G. Jung.

The inevitable reality of aging is a particular difficulty, often an agony, for the Aphrodite-identified woman. The power that Aphrodite wields is gradually being lost, and this is extremely hard to accept, especially when the woman has no other power in herself to rely on. Now she must become something other than Aphrodite or dwindle to a bitter and lonely end. Here is where Sophia, or Wisdom, shines— a vastly greater and more all-encompassing feminine figure than Aphrodite. We will look at the issue of aging and the archetype of Sophia in chapter 7.

In these times, when the idolization of Aphrodite—and the tragedy that ensues—are perhaps more widespread than ever, the crucial key for women is *consciousness*. Hopefully your own consciousness will be expanded by the stories and ideas in this book.

NOTES

[1] Hesiod, *The Homeric Hymns* V, trans. Hugh G. Evelyn-White (Cambridge, MA: Harvard University Press, 1977), p. 407.

[2] *Third Homeric Hymn to Aphrodite*, trans. Charles Boer, 2nd ed. (Dallas, TX: Spring Publications, 1979), p. 83.

[3] James Hillman, "Pink Madness," Spring Audio, Inc.

[4] Homer, *Iliad*, trans. Richmond Lattimore (Chicago: University of Chicago Press, 1961), p. 299.

[5] Hesiod, *Theogony*, trans. Hugh G. Evelyn-White (Kindle Edition, 2009), pp. 205-206.

[6] C.G. Jung, "The Structure of the Psyche," in *The Structure and Dynamics of the Psyche,* vol. 8 of *The Collected Works of C.G. Jung* (hereafter *CW*), 20 vols. (Princeton, NJ: Princeton University Press, 1953-1979), § 414.

[7] Joyce Carol Oates, "Little Bird of Heaven" (New York: Harper Collins, 2000), p. 116.

[8] Andrew Samuels, *A Critical Dictionary of Jungian Analysis* (London: Routledge & Kegan Paul, 1987), p. 26.

[9] Johnny Cash, "Ring of Fire" (Sony Music, 1998).

[10] Edward F. Edinger, *The Eternal Drama: The Inner Meaning of Greek Mythology* (Boston: Shambhala, 1994), p. 44.

[11] Karl Kerenyi, *Goddess of Sun and Moon* (Dallas: Spring Publications, 1979), p. 60.

[12] *Ibid.,* p. 81.

[13] William Faulkner, *Absalom, Absalom* (New York: Random House, 1986), p. 112.

[14] John A. Sanford, *Hate, Love, and Ecstasy* (Wilmette, IL: Chiron, 1995), p. 82.

Chapter 2

Aphrodite's Story:
Films and Novels

> One medieval tale features an outdoorsman named Hilarion out searching for a man wiser than himself, then sitting on a riverbank alone to fish. He meets "a lady beautiful beyond compare, the which for all clothing wore only her own hair golden and exceedingly long." Hilarion asks, "Who art thou, for this forest is haunted by spirits, and I would know whether thou art one of such, and of evil intent, as the demon Venus, or a woman like the mother who bore me."
> —Bradley TePaske, *Sexuality and the Religous Imagination*[1]

Film, literature, and television provide several mediums in which the Aphrodite archetype emerges as lived out in widely diverse settings, time periods, and circumstances. From the escapades of Samantha in *Sex and the City*, to Edie's role as neighborhood vixen in *Desperate Housewives*, to Flaubert's Emma in *Madame Bovary* and Thomas Hardy's Eustacia in *Return of the Native*, the Aphrodite woman never fails to grab the limelight. Whether tragedy follows in her wake depends as much on her ability to draw upon other aspects of her nature as it does on how others react to her. The only sure thing is that the story will have "juice."

Here we will take a closer look at a sampling of Aphrodite characters to see how their development fares in the hands of their creators.

MALÉNA

Maléna is an Italian film (2000) starring Monica Bellucci and Giuseppe Sulfaro. It was directed and written by Giuseppe Tornatore, based on a short story by Luciano Vincenzoni. The film takes place in Fascist Italy during World War II, and the story of Maléna is seen from the point of view of Renato, a boy on the verge of adolescence who worships and adores Maléna for her beauty and virtue. We follow the unfolding of Maléna's narrative through his eyes.

Maléna has been recently abandoned by her husband, who went off to fight the Allied forces in North Africa. She is overwhelmingly beautiful, and now alone and defenseless, inspiring all the men in this primitive and provincial Sicilian town, Castelcuto, to lose their heads over her, and all the women to hate and scorn her for the strong power of her beauty and sexuality. As her days continue as a woman alone, desired by all men and hated by all women, she becomes the subject of town gossip and intrigue. She is an outsider, hailing from another village, and without a husband to protect her, she becomes a pariah figure sequestered and isolated because of her unreal beauty. No one will hire her, so she cannot find a job, and as food rations dwindle, her vulnerable position grows more problematic. Renato spies on her relentlessly and idealizes her as the perfect, pure woman mourning her husband—who is reported dead shortly into the film, having been killed in North Africa. While the other boys in his social gang make vulgar jokes about Maléna's evident sexuality, Renato feels personally offended by their jabs. He worships her like a goddess—she is the one spot of beauty in the barren, parched landscape of Fascist Italy, the one point of light in the impoverished, mean village.

When the townsmen discover that her husband is dead and Maléna is available, they aggressively pursue her, each trying to win her over. One elderly, lecherous dentist claims that Maléna is his fiancée, and takes her to court to try to prove this. Maléna's lawyer points out that Maléna stands guilty of only one thing—her beauty—while the rest of the townspeople seethe with collective jealousy or desire for her. Of course, hours later, her lawyer tries to take advantage of the situation and have her for himself. She refuses him, but after this her reputation spirals downward. More rumors fly that she is a whore, a home-wrecker. A woman yells in the town square, to anyone who will listen, that Maléna was "born a whore." Maléna's father, Signor Bonsignore, a teacher of Latin at the local school, disowns her after receiving an anonymous letter stating that Maléna is sleeping with the whole town and dishonoring her family name.

Without a father or a husband, she falls prey to the town's hatred—men and women who have been itching to accuse and ostracize her from the start. As food shortages and bombings increase, along with an influx of refugees flooding the town, bringing with them the threat of disease, Maléna becomes the palpable "shadow" of the community. All of their fear, dislike, and resentment generated by the war is projected onto her. She becomes the scapegoat, and bears the brunt of their collective loathing.

After an intense bombing session one cloudless afternoon, Maléna's father is found dead under the rubble. She is now utterly alone, devoid of defenders. Driven by the need for food, as well as buckling under the town's oppressive loathing, she gives in to the image that everyone has been waiting for, and transforms herself into their fantasy: a vampish, loose woman with short red hair, red lipstick, and black sheer stockings. She flaunts and struts her beauty in the main square, drawing lustful male stares, vulgar comments, and evoking in the women a vengeful satisfaction that she has finally fallen from grace. No longer the Madonna, she is now a veritable whore. With the arrival of the German soldiers who occupy the town, Maléna sides with them out of a sheer need for survival, and becomes known not only as a prostitute, but a traitorous one.

The end of the war and the liberation of the Sicilian town by the Americans follow—and so does Maléna's ultimate disgrace. In the midst of waving flags and postwar celebrations, the townswomen do not forget who needs to be punished. They immediately drag Maléna out of the hotel, where she has been staying with German officers, and proceed to beat and chastise her, ending with the ultimate punishment of cutting off her now blond locks until she is left a shorn, ashamed, and badly beaten woman, defaced for all to witness.

After her beating, Maléna flees the town and takes the next train to Messina. Days later, her husband, who had been left for dead, returns to Castelcuto. One of his arms has been blown away, but he is alive and looking for Maléna. He asks everyone in the town where she has gone, but no one will look him in the eye. He returns to his old house, only to find that a refugee camp has been established there.

Desperate and confused, he sits down on the church steps, wondering what has happened to his life. Renato, the boy who has been following Maléna and knows where she has gone, hands him a note telling him that he knows the truth about his wife, who remained faithful to him in her heart, and left the town after the war ended.

The husband leaves in search of his wife, taking the train to Messina. A year passes, and in the next scene, Maléna returns to Castelcuto with her husband on her arm, walking modestly through the main square where she once had been ridiculed and tormented. They settle back into the town, and Maléna returns to normal life, reintegrating herself into the fabric of the community. A sense of communal guilt hangs over the townswomen's heads over how harshly and unfairly they had treated Maléna. The women finally begin to accept her. Although Maléna is slightly older and more subdued, she is still beautiful and mysterious, retaining her power even after her public desecration in the square.

The figure of Maléna, in her goddess-like beauty, is intrinsically threatening to both men and women, causing them to turn against her with vehemence. Maléna is an example of a "pure Aphrodite woman," in the sense that she fully embodies the archetype of Aphrodite—inciting envy, anxiety, and fear among the local population. Because she has no other characteristics to temper her Aphrodite nature, she walks through the piazza as a living image of the goddess—and no one knows how to respond to such an event. Confronted with this mysterious, highly erotic image of a woman, the male impulse objectifies her into purely a sexual object, instead of viewing her as a real person who is also a daughter and a widow. Because of this male view of femininity in simplistic, "black-and-white" terms, the town fails to acknowledge Maléna's reality as a human being—as existing simultaneously as a widow and a siren, a Madonna and a whore, as an integrated feminine figure who contains numerous qualities within her psyche.

At the start of the film, although she meets with suspicion from the townswomen, the men still refer to her as a Madonna—a lonely, suffering widow, a martyr to the war effort. But after she is falsely accused of adultery with the dentist and of sleeping with the whole town, Maléna embraces the other extreme, transforming into a declared prostitute by dying her hair a vulgar red, cutting it short, and consorting with the occupying forces. She betrays herself, unable to hold the tension of having both sides within her, and accepts only one aspect of herself, which eventually brings about her shaming in the public square after the Germans are defeated.

One year later, when Maléna returns with her husband to the place of her past shame, one could say that she has in fact integrated these two sides of herself. She is no longer all beauty and sex, but she is also not an old, wizened matron dressed in black. She is still beautiful, but her effect is tempered by the husband on her arm; her subtle, beige-colored dress; and her hair—natural in color and of medium length. When she goes shopping at the local market, women approve of her courage in returning to the village. She moves through the fruit and vegetable stalls with dignity and grace, a living image of a woman who encompasses the myriad aspects of what it means to be one—she is still mysteriously beautiful, but she bravely no longer identifies with just one aspect of her femininity.

After shame and tragedy, the final outcome in this story is positive, even redemptive. But many Aphrodite stories are tragic throughout—not only for the Aphrodite character herself, but also for those she has ensnared through her archetypal power.

Madame Bovary

One story of this type is Gustave Flaubert's *Madame Bovary*. Madame Bovary may be thought of as a materialistic, narcissistic woman who cares only about the next love affair and about adorning herself at the expense of all else. However, if we look at her archetypally, she is born with and caught in the Aphrodite web.

As a young girl in the convent, Emma was enchanted with the many tales she read about princes and princesses and lovers. She had dreams of luxury and impossible love. After her life at the convent, she lived in a modest farmhouse with her father. Her mother was dead. She wondered, where do they come from, the cavaliers who would serenade me? In her imagination, she lived in a world of romance, intrigue, and dangerous love. She found only boredom in the here and now; only what was far away was of value. She wished for a Prince Charming, like Cinderella. She felt disdain for her country life. Of course there were other girls, other pretty girls, who had also been at the convent, and had been exposed to novels about romance and undying love, about Tristan and Isolde. So one cannot really explain Emma in a cause-and-effect or developmental way; it was simply how she was from birth. Her psychic makeup, her "bones," were a certain way, and brought her, in the end, to a dark, painful, self-inflicted death: in despair because the debt she has accumulated will ruin her husband, and refused any help by her two former lovers, she swallows arsenic and dies in agony.

For a while after her death, her husband Charles idealizes the memory of his wife. Eventually, though, he finds her letters from Rodolphe and Leon, her former lovers, and he is forced to confront the truth. He dies alone in his garden, and their daughter Berthe is sent off to work in a cotton mill.

Emma had no other aspects in her psyche to fall back on—it was only romance that energized her—she had no other creative interest and no interest in her little girl, and so Berthe ends up an orphan and a laborer, everything Emma despised. One might say Emma's shadow, her own peasant-class upbringing, fell in spades upon her helpless little daughter.

This brings to mind an Emma Bovary-type woman with whom I have worked. This woman was interested only in clothes, glamorous restaurants and hotels, and romance. She was not capable of sticking with someone—just as Emma was unable to stick to one man. She could easily ensnare men because of her allure, but she got rid of them just as easily when they became boring and stupid to her, just as Charles became to Emma. My patient was finally able to settle down as she approached fifty—not because she had necessarily met the right prince, but she was worn out and almost tired of having the next intense relationship. She also appreciated the fact that she did have someone to hang out with, go to movies with, and that—yes—this meant she would not be all alone as she became older and older. She had found someone who would put up with her, and she knew she was hard to be with on a daily basis—she spent a lot of money, had dark, angry moods, and was not often able to compromise. Like Emma, she often felt dark and lifeless—however, when a man, perhaps at the supermarket, would flirt with her, she would spark up and life would be worth living again, at least for the moment. Through writing down her dreams, painting her dreams, and working faithfully week after week in analysis, she developed other aspects of her personality over time—which Emma, who brought all around her to ruin, had not been able to do.

THOMAS HARDY NOVELS

The type of man who is particularly prone to becoming ensnared by an Aphrodite woman, and to come to ruin thereby, is illustrated in two novels by Thomas Hardy: *The Return of the Native* and *Jude the Obscure*.

Clym, in *Return of the Native*, has given up his business career in Paris to return to his hometown in England. He wants to be a schoolteacher to those who can't afford existing schools. Eustacia, who hears of his return, becomes fascinated by him and her idea of his likely return to Paris—which is where *she* wants to go; who would stay on Egdon Heath if they could go to Paris? Eustacia begins to meet Clym out on the heath, and soon he falls in love with her, despite his mother's disapproval. Clym, the humanitarian, is no match for the willful and restless Eustacia. His former closeness to his mother does not shield him, and he leaves his mother's house and decides to marry Eustacia. They marry, and for a time live a secluded life on the heath. But when Clym must cease his studies to be a schoolteacher because of severe eye trouble and becomes a lowly furze cutter on the heath, Eustacia's dreams of social status and perhaps someday a Parisian life are shattered, and she begins to involve herself again with Wildeve, her former lover.

Clym and his mother tragically miss encountering each other when they are both trying to pursue a reconciliation. His mother is not admitted to Clym's house—Eustacia is there with Wildeve—and is bitten by a snake on her long walk back home, and shortly thereafter dies. The sudden death of his mother throws Clym into an illness, but when he recovers, he finds out what really happened that day, and that is seemingly the end of his relationship with Eustacia, who leaves to return to her grandfather's house.

Later, Eustacia, having accepted Wildeve's offer to help her get to Paris, leaves her grandfather's house before seeing a letter from Clym offering reconciliation. Late on that dark, stormy night, they start searching for her—but before they can prevent it she throws herself into a stream, and even though she is pulled out, she does not survive. Clym ends up utterly alone, becoming an itinerant preacher of moral lectures.

Compared to the other male characters in the story, there is a certain softness and one-sidedness to Clym, a lack of relationship to the darker side of things, and it is perhaps these qualities that brand him as likely Aphrodite prey.

Jude, in *Jude the Obscure*, was ensnared by women from beginning to end—not only by the Aphrodite types, Arabella and Sue, but also by Drusilla, the aged aunt who brought him up after the death of his parents. Jude is helpless against them, so trapped by his mother complex that he has no sharp psychological sword to brandish; he is possessed by his anima. Jude is a "mother's son," Eros-driven rather than Logos-driven. He has a poor relationship with his own inner feminine aspects, and this complex so overwhelms his ego that he identifies with it and is lost in the darkness—the nonreflection—of that identification.

Arabella is the fruit that Eros-driven men are compelled to eat. She is forbidden (or so Jude perceives her to be), and she lures Jude to herself as bait. Mothers' sons are compelled to eat, to take a bite of poison in the guise of a seductive woman, whereas Logos-driven men, more concerned with power, can often easily say no. Jude is enchanted; he is trapped permanently under the spell of the feminine—be it Arabella or the maiden, Sue Bridehead.

Neither woman provides any relief to Jude's anguish—and indeed, for most of the novel they only amplify his suffering, his obscurity, and his poverty on all levels. Arabella is of the flesh and Sue is of the phantom soul; as a combined force in Jude's life they lead to the death of his body and soul. In Jungian terms, both aspects of his anima are negative and destructive and lead to his psychic death, for he is possessed by those aspects of the anima embodied in these two women.

Jude is close to a suffering modern male in his psychological and spiritual makeup. He is alienated from himself and from any form of real intimacy or authentic relationship with either woman, a man torn asunder from beginning to end. He also is like a failed modern male in the fact that he is unable to know, even on his deathbed, that he has lived a worthy life and fulfilled his destiny. Instead he blindly enacts the dictates of his archetypal engraving, lacking the consciousness and the ego strength to alter this innate pattern.

This story reminds me of a somewhat typical male patient who falls for an Aphrodite-type woman. This forty-five-year-old, never married man referred to himself as "the slug" and had even written stories about a man who was a slug. He worked as a massage therapist and had very little money. He was always looking for the perfect woman, and had many Internet dates. This pattern had gone on for over twenty years. He was basically a mild man, or what I would call a "pink" man—one who is passive-aggressive and a pushover, with a mean streak. He is the first one to assist the hostess clear the table at a dinner party, always helpful, as opposed to a Zeus-type man who would not consider getting up to lend a hand, but would be talking with other men about "investment deals," smoking a cigar, and drinking expensive after-dinner drinks. Often "pink" men are in professions where they are of service, rather than being served. Again and again the women with whom he had brief flings—not more than six weeks—would end up bossing him around; he was passive and thus would find women who were the opposite; quite often they were very aggressive.

His last girlfriend was a prostitute he met in Oaxaca. She, of course, convinced him that she was in love with him and that he was special. It was apparent from the description of her that she had the ability to capture and get what she wanted from many, many men. She made them believe that she had had to drop out of school and support her family, that she had a "heart of gold"—what she wanted and got was their gold. She brought him to her family's home—or what appeared to be her family—outside of the city. He bought her very expensive gold jewelry and stayed with her an extra week, treating her to a posh five-star hotel. All of this was on his credit card; he was over seventy thousand dollars in debt. After being home for about a month, he went back to see her again. After receiving more jewelry from him, she showed him her box of gold, filled to the top—gifts from her many sweethearts. He came a third time, but she then disappeared, and he could no long find her or reach her by phone, even though they were supposedly planning to marry. He called and left message after message at the cathouse where he had met her.

He did not last more than six months in his analysis. He had few dreams, and sadly was not able to build up his masculine strength and focus on himself in an in-depth, meaningful way. He could not do the work; evidently he had been to a number of therapists before finding me.

Characters such as Emma Bovary and Eustacia in Thomas Hardy's *Return of the Native* bring men to ruin because, totally autoerotic in their possession by the Aphrodite archetype, they are incapable of real relationship. They may appear to be relating—especially to the men who pursue them—but in actuality they relate to their own idealized selves. The men are useful to them only as they mirror and support the glorious, irresistible Aphrodite self-image.

These Aphroditic characters show up often in novels, plays, opera, and films because the trajectory of their tragedies creates such great theater. As soon as such a character appears in a story—such as Blanche in *A Streetcar Named Desire*, or Gloria in the film *Butterfield 8*—we say to ourselves, "This is not going to end well!" and of course it doesn't, although we relish the drama of every tragic step. This drama is what stories are made of—they can be considered "cautionary tales"—but there are also many real-life tragedies that grow out of possession by the Aphrodite archetype. Some are known only within families and neighborhoods, but when a celebrity is involved, Aphrodite makes the news!

NOTES

[1] Bradley A. TePaske, *Sexuality and the Religious Imagination* (New Orleans, LA: Spring Journal Books, 2008), p. 203, citing Helen Meredith Garth, *Saint Mary Magdalene in Medieval Literature* (Baltimore, MD: Johns Hopkins University Press, 1950), pp. 23-24.

Chapter 3

Aphrodite in the Spotlight— Actresses, Celebrities, and the Dark Side of Hollywood

"I'm glad it's over with now..."
—Leona Gage[1]

I now come to modern-day Hollywood and Beverly Hills, home to countless contemporary daughters of Aphrodite. Hollywood, as we know, is the principal seat of the motion picture and television film industries. Filmmaker Thom Anderson refers to the image of Hollywood as rootless, evil, banal, and morally corrupt. The history of Hollywood dates back to 1853, when the first home in the area, an adobe, was built. Hollywood's original name was Edendale. The pioneers of the motion picture industry found Southern California desirable because of the mild temperatures, the varied terrain, and the labor market. In 1908, one of the first moving pictures telling a story, *The Count of Monte Cristo*, was finished in the Hollywood area.

Beverly Hills developed as an urban community entirely in the twentieth century. Formed as a city in 1914, the population of Beverly Hills soared between 1922 and 1930 with the boom in the motion picture industry. According to a friend who is a fine-art dealer on Rodeo Drive, just steps away from what was home to me as a child, Beverly Hills is the devil's playground. Anything that reminds one of death, one's mortal end and the passing of time, does not sell. Death, rot, and decay do not sell. Yet some of the inhabitants, in their pursuit of youth and beauty, perhaps look more mummified than those who live anyplace else on the planet.

There are many shadows in Beverly Hills and Hollywood. In proceeding, I will share thoughts and feelings with you from a depth-psychological standpoint and from the personal standpoint of one who was born with Aphrodite engraved in her psyche, grew up in Beverly Hills, and worked in Hollywood.

I was brought up about a mile from Greystone Mansion, which the *Los Angeles Times* described as "a monument to sun-drenched dreams of wealth and power, [where] shadows of mystery and scandal still lurk."[1] Greystone Mansion was built by Edward Doheny, who lived in Los Angeles in dire poverty in a run-down boarding house until he struck oil from a well he dug himself near the current Belmont High School in Los Angeles. Tragedy struck this rags-to-riches family when Ned Doheny, 35-year-old heir to the family fortune, was shot through the head. Nearby was the body of his trusted secretary, also shot dead. To this day the unsolved crime is a source of rumor and speculation. In 1954 Lucy Doheny, the mother of Ned, sold the property to Paul Trousdale, who developed it as the Trousdale Estates—where I lived with my parents, and where Elvis lived with Priscilla, and Lisa Marie Presley was born. In one of our family stories, my father was driving down Benedict Canyon, very near the Trousdale Estates, when his car swerved as a tire went flat. Elvis, driving by, pulled over and changed the tire on my father's Lincoln.

Many years have passed since I lived on the estates that were once Ned Doheny's. His castle-like estate has loomed over Beverly Hills since 1928. In my late teens I dated a Doheny heir, who, like myself, was to become heir to a dark, melancholy, and fateful event. Murder strikes home with me, for murder has touched my life in a profound way. Both my father and brother (my only sibling) were killed at their place of business in Beverly Hills, some years ago. Like the Doheny murder, this double murder remains unsolved by the Beverly Hills police and shrouded in mystery. It is even possible that a close male relative of mine may have paid the murderer to pull the trigger. This powerful dark event coincided with the emergence of a new level of soul inside of me; I was admitted into the training program at the Los Angeles Jung Institute six weeks after the murder of my brother, Harry, who is seven years younger than I, and my father Julius. I am still trying to make sense psychologically of these dark events in my family and my fate that have so penetrated my essence.

As a young Aphrodite woman I worked in Hollywood as a dancer, model, actor, and movie extra, straight out of Central Casting. During my teens and twenties I worked on hundreds of television shows and films—from *Twist around the Clock*, surfing commercials, *Viva Las Vegas* and *Harum Scarum* with Elvis, *Ozzie and Harriet*, *Dr. Kildare*, *Ben Casey*, and *Love American Style*. As a girl on the set, I was asked out by Elvis. I declined, knowing at the time that it was not a real date but that I would be picked up by one of his Memphis hometown boys—flunky gofers, bodyguards, friends of Elvis, and procurers of women. Elvis simply had sex with the young girls, and then the gofer would drive the girl home in one of Elvis's limos. I was also asked to pose nude for an issue of *Playboy* called "Extras in Hollywood"—which I also declined. Neither "opportunity" offered the kind of limelight that my Aphrodite soul was fervently seeking in those days. Worse, as a mere extra and dancer, I was in the underbelly of usable, disposable Hollywood girls. Still, there was always the possibility of being recognized as a star—a lure whose power I felt until the emptiness of the pursuit engulfed me.

Some cities carry more darkness than others, but for me, Beverly Hills is the darkest. It is also the capital of Aphrodite citizens. Thebes is the dark city of ancient Greece. In Thebes, Antigone's brother Polyneices was killed. Antigone, moved by the love of her brother, buried him secretly and performed his funeral service. (I too performed the funeral service for my brother and my father.) Beverly Hills, like Thebes, calls to mind another city festering in darkness. In Dostoevsky's *Crime and Punishment*, Raskolnikov, a poor student, murders a St. Petersburg pawnbroker and her younger sister Elana. Raskolnikov's emotions torment him, and he struggles with his feverish conscience and his mounting sense of horror as he wanders the city's miserable, polluted, hot, crowded streets. My father too was a pawnbroker, though a so-called high-class pawnbroker, who loaned money to many film and rock stars as well as princes and princesses. He once gave me a diamond and turquoise ring that belonged to an Egyptian princess. Like Raskolnikov, the person who killed my father and brother was enraged at them for some past transgression regarding

loaning money and redeeming jewelry. My father died within an hour
of the crime; my brother, three months later. I can easily bring to mind
the image of Raskolnikov's "hands . . . sticky with blood."[3]

Working in Hollywood in my younger years, especially as a "stand-
in," had already made me feel like a disenfranchised, crushed orphan.
Little did I know to what degree I would actually become an
orphan. Of all the jobs, the "stand-in" is, I think, the darkest and
most shadow-like. A stand-in for an actor is literally his or her
shadow. Usually the person is chosen because of a slight
resemblance, like being blond if the star is blond, and being of
similar height and build. He or she wears a sweater or coat of the
color the actor is going to wear for the scene while the crew lights
the set. One stands there hour after hour, day after day, year after
year—a fill-in, an object that only stands for the real thing.
Sometimes well-known actors or stars are loyal to their stand-ins
and include them in their contracts, but other times, even after
the passage of a year, the famous one does not even know the name
of the stand-in. Being a double or a stand-in is light years away
from the real thing, and it does not feel very good—especially for
an Aphrodite type who thrives on stunning others. I had other
parts where I worked as a dancer, a choreographer, a minor actor,
and an extra—for example, as a nurse on *Dr. Kildare*. These sorts of
jobs were not too bad, as I did fill some sort of role, no matter how
small. But being a stand-in—which can be the steadiest job if one
works for an entire movie, or goes on location with the star, or even
works for years and years on a TV series—this was the worst, the most
objectifying. At my best, I felt jealous and envious; at my worst, in
the depths of despair.

On the set the men would flirt with me rather a lot, and that is
what sent me into analysis. It was not only the boring misery of the
dark, gloomy sets, but repeatedly I would be asked, "Why aren't you
smiling?" This was intolerable. At the time I did not know the words
for what I was feeling and experiencing. I was suffering from a profound
sense of emptiness over the lack of meaning in my life. Jungian analysis
is an excellent means for dealing with just such a sense of
meaninglessness. Without analysis my life might have spiraled into
the underworld—without the inner wisdom I discovered in my

personal analytic work, I may have turned to drugs, or a sort of prostitution, or even died young.

THE TRAGIC BLONDE

Aphroditic young women have flocked to Hollywood for many years. Often they are blondes. Hollywood has a fascination with tragic, dead blondes. Thom Anderson's 2003 film *Los Angeles Plays Itself* opens with a stripper with long blond hair being hit by a car. Dead blondes include Jayne Mansfield, Marilyn Monroe, Grace Kelly, Jean Seberg, Jean Harlow, Anna Nicole Smith, and many others. In an episode of the HBO series *Carnivale*, a young hoochy-koochy dancer—whose blond mother is a prostitute and whose father is her mother's pimp— dreams of making it in Hollywood. The first thing she does is bleach her hair blond. The most current blond "it girl" is Paris Hilton (although her spotlight is fading), heir to a hotel fortune, referred to as "party girl" of the new century. A *Vanity Fair* contributor describes her: "There's something magnetic about her. I think she's beautiful. Part of the reason is the sensation of scandal around her. You know, she's sort of a bad girl, she always has this sexy look on her face."[4] A tape of Paris having sex in a Las Vegas hotel room was being offered for sale all over the Internet. With a given name like Paris, what does one do anyway? Perhaps blondes carry the Aphrodite archetype even more than their raven-haired sisters; Aphrodite is, after all, golden.

Often Aphrodite women die earlier than other women, but after having many husbands. Rita Hayworth, for example, married Orson Welles, Prince Aly Khan, and singer Dick Haymes, among others, and endured spousal abuse, drinking problems, and a sad death at age sixty-nine. Said the *L.A. Times*: "Bestowed by Hollywood with the surreal title 'The Love Goddess,' Hayworth was one of the greatest sex symbols of the 1940s and '50s. But as with so many of Hollywood's leading ladies—from Clara Bow to Marilyn Monroe—Hayworth never found the love, security or meaning in her personal life that she so desperately sought."[5] Novelist Joseph Roth hauntingly describes the deep waters for an aging beauty:

> But old age was approaching with cruel, hushed steps and
> sometimes in crafty disguises. She counted the days slipping
> past her, and every morning, the fine wrinkles, delicate webs

that old age had spun at night around her innocently sleeping
eyes. Yet her heart was that of a sixteen-year-old girl. Blessed
with constant youth, it dwelled in the middle of the aging body,
a lovely secret in a ruinous castle. Every young man whom Frau
von Taussig took in her arms was the guest she had so long been
yearning for.[6]

On one level these women had abundant opportunities: beauty,
money, power, adulation. Yet, like Princess Diana, they could not fulfill
their promise. Diana, who was very attracted to Hollywood and
vacationed with Goldie Hawn and Kurt Russell, for example, died
young. I was angry when I heard about her death. She was a woman
who could have been queen, could have achieved so many important
things. She did significant charitable work and desired to soothe the
suffering of others—people afflicted with AIDS, leprosy, and the
mutilated victims of land mines. Nevertheless, she died with her lover
of forty days and forty nights. Her Persephone-like, Aphroditic ways
appeared to run the archetypal show. The myth of Persephone recounts
how youthful Persephone was gathering roses and lilies, crocuses and
violets, and narcissus in a lush meadow when the earth gaped open
and Pluto, Lord of the Dead, issuing forth from the abyss, carried her
off on his golden cart to be his bride and queen in the gloomy
subterranean world. Princess Diana, like Persephone, went down with
her dark lover into the subterranean underworld tunnel, in her modern
chariot, and died. Down, down they sped. Barry Hillenbrand writes:
"Some saw the Princess martyred by publicity, hounded unto death
by the cameras that loved her so and that then feasted on her funeral."[7]
However, if Diana had had some Hestia qualities available in her
psyche she might have been at home, tending the hearth in some way,
and she would not have created so much allure, attraction, and
fascination for the paparazzi. Hestia may be lovely but she is not
fascinating. Or, if she had had some Hera in her bones, she would
have just stayed married and been jealous of Camilla, but she also would
have defended the proprieties of marriage.

For Diana, as for so many women, romance—especially romance
that is new—has an autonomous force that one feels compelled to obey.
Once Cupid's arrow penetrates and wounds some women, they find
it almost impossible to say no. Only the strongest can resist the
pull of one more love affair. It is perhaps only through one's quest

for meaning that one can get out of the Aphrodite trap. Diana's life was like a fairy tale. One mourner inscribed, "You were a Cinderella at the Ball and now you are a Sleeping Beauty." At Diana's funeral, Elton John sang *Candle in the Wind*, a song he had originally written for Marilyn Monroe.

Yet another tragic obituary: platinum-blond actress Lana Clarkson was found dead inside Phil Spector's Alhambra castle on February 3, 2002. Clarkson, a forty-year-old actress, boasted that she had been inspired by Marilyn Monroe. According to one of her friends, "Lana had that sort of '50s movie-star quality. She definitely saw herself as that type of royalty." However, she remained stuck in an early Marilyn rut of low-budget, occasionally topless roles such as *Amazon Women on the Moon*, *Barbarian Queen 1*, and *Barbarian Queen 2*. She also did TV commercials for K-mart. Detectives tried to figure out how Clarkson met Specter and wound up dead on the floor of his home after accepting a very late-night ride in the music producer's Mercedes (some years later, Spector was convicted of her murder). The killing left Clarkson's friends mourning a woman they described as indomitable, yet increasingly aware of the difficulties older actresses face. The song playing on Clarkson's website before she was killed was a Steely Dan hit called "Peg." The lyrics go: "I've seen your picture / your name in lights above it / it's like a dream come true. / And when you smile for the camera / I know they're gonna love it…" Tragedy is not how one dies but what kind of life one has lived.

Another tragic blonde is one who became a porn star. As a young woman, Marilyn Chambers moved to Los Angeles for film work. She did not receive any roles except for a low-budget film in which she appeared nude. Depressed, she left Los Angeles for San Francisco, where she held several jobs, including work as a topless model and a "bottomless" dancer. During her early career, perhaps her most visible modeling job was as the "cover girl" on the Ivory Snow soap box, posing as the mother holding the baby under the tag line "100% pure." Later, although she had not planned to, she agreed to act in a porn film. After filming concluded, she informed the producers that she was "the Ivory Snow Girl," and they quickly capitalized on this by billing her as the "100% pure" girl in other adult films. Nearly every film she made following this incident featured a cameo of her on the Ivory Snow box.

In her subsequent career, she was noted for her enthusiastic performances of deep throat, anal, lesbian, interracial, and double or triple penetration scenes. She was one of the first female stars to shave her pubic hair, a practice now routine for porn actresses. Later in her career, she had a series of breast augmentations raising her from a B-cup to at least a D. She was reputedly one of the first porn actresses to have her genitals pierced.

Her first marriage ended after the release of the film *Behind the Green Door*. Her second marriage was to porn producer/director/manager Chuck Traynor, who was formerly married to Linda Lovelace. After that marriage ended, Chambers married her third husband, truck driver Tom Taylor. She died in her trailer park home, of drug and alcohol abuse, on April 13, 2009, at age fifty-six. Chambers is another Hollywood blond who died, isolated, at an early age.

Amy Winehouse, in her brief and tragic life, appears to be an Aphrodite type judging by her outrageously sexy dress, leopard tops, and exaggerated long-hair extensions and eye makeup. However, she seems to be more a Persephone-like visitor from the underworld, briefly roaming about our world in search of peace, but finding only torment.

Anna Nicole Smith is the quintessential Marilyn Monroe/Jayne Mansfield type. However, she is the light that makes one squint. I always winced at her images—they were glaringly exaggerated. To me, she was not the "upper-air golden one" but a living, breathing testament to the distortion of the Aphrodite heritage. Her name was Vickie Lynn Hogan and she was born in Harris County, Texas. She dropped out of high school, worked in a fried chicken joint, and had her first child when she was seventeen. Moving to Houston, she found successive sources of employment working at Walmart, as a waitress at Red Lobster, and then as a stripper. In a Houston strip club she met oil tycoon Howard Marshall; she was twenty-six and he was eighty-nine. Shortly thereafter, she saw an ad in a newspaper to audition for *Playboy* magazine, and the rest became part of tabloid history. After Marshall died, Anna Nicole spiraled down over the years and was involved in a much-published court battle in an attempt to gain her husband's estate. When her infant daughter was born, at least four men claimed to be the father, and all said they'd had long-term affairs with Anna Nicole, including Zsa Zsa Gabor's husband.

Anna Nicole died of drug overdoses. Before her body was buried, it began decomposing at a very fast pace. Reasons for her more rapid decomposition were the drugs found in her body at the autopsy, the legal battles that delayed her embalming until over a week after her death, and the nearly month-long wait for her burial in the warm Bahamas weather. She, who had devoted her entire short life to creating an appearance that was desired by all, underwent the ravages of the underworld in her death, rendering her appearance a horrific sight that necessitated a closed-casket funeral. Anna Nicole is yet another sad story of pure celebrity—a young woman who was a victim of the love goddess and appeared to have little else but her beauty and voluptuous figure to rely upon. She was forty years old when she died in the Hard Rock Hotel.

CELEBRITIES ADORED AS GODDESSES

She has graced the covers of glossy magazines and has been the subject of pop art, but now Kate Moss has been immortalized in 18-carat gold. A gold statue of the supermodel, worth $1.5 million, was unveiled at the British Museum in 2008. The work, entitled *Siren*, was created by sculptor Marc Quinn. The statue of Moss, who is described as an "Aphrodite of our times," now stands in the British Museum's Nereid Gallery, alongside legendary Greek heroines such as the *Crouching Venus*, a statue of Venus caught bathing. The sculpture, which is hollow, weighs about as much as the supermodel herself, according to the artist, and is believed to be the largest gold statue made in the world since Ancient Egyptian times. Quinn said of his choice of Moss as a subject: "I thought the next thing to do would be to make a sculpture of the person who's the ideal beauty of the moment. Divinity lives on." Is this not a current act of worship and homage to a modern-day goddess? When this was done in past ages, the person making the prayer or offering would hope to please the god or goddess and persuade him or her to look favorably on the person's wants and desires.

In ancient times, statues and figures of Aphrodite came in all sizes. Some were life-sized or larger, and others were modest representations meant to adorn a single small room. In Cyprus, there were annual processions and festivals in her honor, and the Cypriots practiced daily worship. The temple owned over one thousand slaves and courtesans, and thus attracted large numbers of sailors and merchants, who visited often and made the city rich. The ancient temples are now museums and places for fashion exhibitions. This brings to mind fashion week, which is played out in the great cities of the world, where magnificent models present themselves and the clothing of famous designers in a yearly ritual. Victoria's Secret is perhaps the most revered of all the shows, featuring the most beautiful women in the world wearing the most revealing clothing as they process down the runway.

That these people happen to be among the world's most beautiful does little to diminish the surreal dimensions of the event. Victoria's Secret fashion show is a died-and-gone-to-heaven dream for some people. Backstage at the shows, the atmosphere is always so frenetic and focused, the deadlines so tight, the volume of tasks to complete so improbable within the time allowed, that Eros is the last thing on anybody's mind. But the public worship the false gods and goddesses, at least during fashion week.

One of the most striking images of this worship of beauty and celebrity is seen in the story of Lola Montes. Born in Ireland in 1821 as Eliza Rosanna Gilbert, she was a dancer and actress who became famous as a Spanish dancer, courtesan, and mistress of King Ludwig I of Bavaria, who made her Countess of Landsfeld. In the 1955 film, *Lola Montes* directed by Max Ophuls, one of the first lines in the film that tells her story is "A femme fatale cannot stay." No matter whom she attracts and seduces, whether she is completely impoverished or living in a palace as she did with Ludwig I of Bavaria, she becomes bored and leaves. Her lovers are intellectuals, kings, very young men, almost anyone. She had an affair with Franz Liszt, who introduced her to the circle of George Sand. At the end of this amazing film, she is reduced to being a circus performer who performs acts from her own famous, notorious life. However, at this stage of her life she is older, very sick, and forced by the ringmaster to attempt life-threatening trapeze acts. When he finally sees that she can no longer perform dangerous high-wire stunts, he puts her into a cage next to the wild animals at his circus. In the cage she sits in her finery, and the ratty public—men from age sixteen and on—are allowed to touch her hand or forehead for a dollar each in a bizarre act of homage. The ringmaster cries out to the crowd that she has been with the kings of Europe and aristocrats, and now you may touch her for a dollar. In this ugly and degrading scenario, she is almost cult-like in the worship she inspires—but her face has a transcendent quality. Even the circus ringmaster, played by Peter Ustinov in the film, remarks at the end that "she gave her body but kept her soul."

Martine Carol, who played Lola Montes in the film, was also a siren, and married four times. One of her husbands was Stephen Crane, American actor and restaurant manager, previously Lana Turner's husband. If Lola was known more for her affairs than her dancing ability, Martine was known more for her glamour than her acting talent. One of the most beautiful women in film, she was frequently cast as an elegant blond seductress. During the late 1940s and early 1950s she was the leading sex symbol and a top box office draw. Despite her fame and considerable fortune, Martine Carol's personal life was filled with turmoil that included a suicide attempt and drug abuse. She died of a heart attack in a Monte Carlo hotel room at the age of forty-six.

The Aphrodite-woman's terrible hunger for the adulation given to a goddess is well illustrated by the story of Leona Gage. In 1957, she was named Miss USA in the precursor to the Miss Universe pageant, but she lost the title the next day when pageant officials learned that she was married and had two children. She had also lied about her age, saying that she was twenty-one although she was eighteen. "I'm glad it's over with now," she told reporters. "I knew the Miss Universe rules forbade a married girl from entering the contest, but I thought I had a chance. I took it and lost." Leona took advantage of the attention that came with losing her tiara and made many television appearances, including one on *The Ed Sullivan Show*. She subsequently pursued an acting career, but it did not take off. Her life after that was difficult. She had six failed marriages and lost custody of her five children, two of whom died before her. She died of heart failure in 2010 at the age of seventy-one.[8]

An exception to this pattern of tragic lives is the life of Janice Rule. She was also an actress in films, and a Broadway dancer remembered for her performance in *Picnic*, who died at the age of seventy-two. For some years, she studied psychoanalysis and earned a doctorate in 1983 from the Southern California Psychoanalytic Institute. She had a private practice in New York City. Rule married three times, suggesting that she carried a strong Aphrodite identification, but it is likely that her analysis afforded her a larger purview of existence, and that she incorporated the traits of other goddesses in her psychology. The story of those other goddesses is our next concern.

NOTES

[1] Her obituary appeared in the *New York Times*, October 11, 2010.

[2] David Colker, *Los Angeles Times*, October 23, 2003.

[3] Fyodor Dostoevsky, *Crime and Punishment*, trans. Jesse Coulson, ed. George Gibian (New York: Norton Critical Edition, 1989), pp. 68-69.

[4] Krista Smith in *Vanity Fair*, October 2005.

[5] Gerald Faris, "Love Goddess of the '40s Dies," *Los Angeles Times*, May 16, 1987.

[6] Joseph Roth, *The Radetzky March* (New York: Overlook TP, 2002), p. 43.

[7] Barry Hillenbrand, *Time*, Commemorative Issue, September 15, 1997, p. 39.

[8] Her obituary appeared in the *New York Times*, October 11, 2010.

Chapter 4

The Classical Aphrodite
and Her Sisters

"Great Lady, you must be one of the gods coming to visit my
house here, Artemis or Leto or the golden Aphrodite or noble
Themis or bright-eyed Athena."[1]

—Hesiod

The earliest descriptions of Aphrodite in classical literature come
from the poetry of Hesiod and Homer, whose poems tell us of
Aphrodite's radiant beauty, her powerful influence over
humans and gods alike, her lovers, and her children. Hesiod and
Homer were thought to have lived in the eighth century B.C.E., possibly
even earlier in Homer's case, and their writing is some of the oldest
known poetry to come down to us from the ancient Greek world.
Numerous other Greek and Roman writers, among them the
playwright Euripides and the poet Sappho, continued to add to
Aphrodite's mythology over the centuries, but it is Hesiod's long poem,
Theogony, and a series of "hymns" attributed to Homer that tell us
the story of Aphrodite's origins.

Hesiod's account of Aphrodite's birth is the version that is
probably most familiar to modern readers: according to the *Theogony*,
Aphrodite emerged from the ocean in a swirl of sea foam, as noted
earlier—the Greek word for foam is *aphros*—as a fully formed goddess.
In this version, her parents were the Earth, a protective, nurturing
mother whom Hesiod called Gaia, and Heaven, a fearsome, brutish

character called Uranus who was despised by Gaia and their children. One night, Uranus wanted to have sex with Gaia, and as he enveloped her, his vengeful son Cronus cut off Uranus's genitals and flung them into the sea, where a "colorless foam" rose up around them. Out of this foam "a maiden grew," and she drifted past the island of Cythera and then to Cyprus, where she came ashore. Hesiod calls her "the inspiring and beautiful goddess" and tells us that she was called Aphrodite "because she was born from the spume of the sea," and also that she was "genital-loving, because she had sprung from sexual organs."[2]

Homer offers a different version of Aphrodite's birth in the *Iliad*, the epic poem of the Trojan War, where Aphrodite is said to be the granddaughter of Gaia and Uranus, and the daughter of Zeus and Dione, a Titan goddess. Despite these differing tales of her beginnings, her place on Mount Olympus as the goddess of love and fertility was secure. Classics scholar Vinciane Pirenne-Delforge wrote that the ancient Greeks accepted this duality in her origins and viewed her as having come from both Greece and the islands farther to the east. Perhaps her eastern origins near Cyprus lent her an exotic quality that made her all the more alluring. The ancient Greeks knew that she belonged in the pantheon of powerful gods.[3]

From Hesiod and Homer's poems we learn of the particular qualities that Aphrodite both personified and encouraged: coy girlishness, an ability to inspire intense feelings of desire and love, and the delight of indulging in pleasure. Homer often describes her as "laughter-loving."[4] In the *Theogony* she is welcomed at once into the pantheon of gods, and Hesiod describes her as inspiring a sense of desire that was difficult, if not impossible, to escape: "This was the destined business she played among men and immortals / Maidenly whispers and smiles and giggles and girlish deception / Pleasure exquisitely pleasant and love that is sweeter than honey."[5] The sixth of the Homeric hymns describes how when she first arrived at Cyprus, blown across the sea by the west wind on a cloud of foam, Aphrodite was welcomed by the Hours, or seasons, and dressed in "ambrosial garments,"[6] a golden crown, and other finery. They then presented her to the rest of the gods, who were so captivated by her loveliness that each of the male gods implored her to marry him. She is praised for her always-smiling face that has the flush of love in it, and she is recounted as kindly bestowing her gifts upon humans.

Just as frequently she personified the sufferings and complications of love. She used trickery and sometimes a petulant tempestuousness to fool other gods and humans into doing her bidding, and she was subject to feelings of guilt and humiliation just like the mortals she sometimes pursued.

In the fifth Homeric hymn, she is described as provoking longing in the gods, and taming humans as well as every other living thing with the gifts of her beauty. This hymn actually begins with an explanation of the three people—the *only* three, Homer makes clear—over whom Aphrodite has no power. These three—Athena, Artemis, and Hestia—are goddesses whose attributes and interests are quite different from Aphrodite's. They are described as being beyond the reach of Aphrodite's charms because, essentially, they have no use for them. Athena is a warrior and the patroness of, as Homer puts it, the "arts of the home."[7] Artemis is a hunter and described as being basically too wild to be tamed by Aphrodite's more feminine wiles. Hestia is described in one translation of the poem as a "pure maiden"[8] and in another, more frankly, as "a spinster."[9] She refused the romantic overtures of both Poseidon and Apollo and vowed to thereafter remain a virgin. We will return to describing these "sisters" of Aphrodite further on.

After presenting these three goddesses, however, the poem goes on to tell of Aphrodite's tremendous power over all other gods and humans. She held great sway over even Zeus, making him often forget his beautiful wife Hera while he romanced mortal women and the occasional adolescent boy. In return, though, Zeus planted in Aphrodite the desire to be with a mortal man, and so she too became swept up in her desire for a human, a young shepherd called Anchises. She seduced him, filling him with love so that he took her to bed immediately. Homer made it clear that it was not only her stunning appearance but her words and manner of speaking that captivated the young man. When Anchises woke, he discovered that she was not a mortal woman but a goddess, and was afraid that he would become impotent, the apparent punishment for a man who slept with an immortal. But Aphrodite told him she would bear him a son called

Aeneas, who would grow up to become the Trojan hero of the *Iliad* and Virgil's epic poem the *Aeneid*. His name, however, refers to the grief and shame Aphrodite felt at having gone to bed with a mortal man. She warns him never to tell anyone about their dalliance and commands him to "Beware the wrath of the gods."[10]

Aphrodite's two great loves were Ares, the god of war and brother of her husband Hephaestus, and Adonis, a beautiful young man from Cyprus, Aphrodite's ancestral home. Aphrodite was married to Hephaestus, another child of Zeus, and the god of fire and metalworking, but she fell in love with his better-looking brother Ares and devoted herself to him instead. In Homer's *Odyssey*, the story is told of how Hephaestus quite literally caught Aphrodite and Ares together, drawing them both up in a fishing net for all the rest of the gods to see—and jeer at. Adonis, being mortal, met a different end. In Ovid's *Metamorphoses*, Adonis is out hunting and dies after being attacked by a wild boar. After his death, Aphrodite is said to have transformed his blood into the rose or, in some versions, the sea anemone, a demonstration of her role as a goddess of fertility and growth. Adonis's death can also be viewed as a reflection of Aphrodite's rivalry with the goddess Artemis, one of the three goddesses over whom she had no power.

Because one of Aphrodite's chief roles as a goddess was to inspire passionate love, those who denied themselves or others the experience of sexual desire would find themselves in trouble with her. It was her job to bring lovers together, for better or worse, and her "wrath" surfaced when she was denied the chance to fulfill this purpose. It surfaced specifically when a human or god rejected the love of another, as in the case of Narcissus, the beautiful young man who fell in love with his own reflection and wasted away while he pined after his own image, never attaining real love. Narcissus ended up in such a state because he snubbed the affections of a nymph who loved him, and so Aphrodite punished him.

Two of the best-known occasions on which Aphrodite intervened in the lives of humans take place in Euripides' *Hippolytus* and in Homer's *Iliad*. In both instances, she persuaded and manipulated the mortals of the story into pursuing passion against their own best interests, and then, later, even against their own wills. It is important to remember that Aphrodite's manipulative charms are an indispensable part of her role as the goddess of love. In classical literature she embodied the pleasure of passionate love, but also the irrational and often destructive forces that can accompany that passion. The poets and playwrights of the classical world knew that in order to tell a good story, they should not only make use of Aphrodite's ability to inspire pleasure, but also, in the interest of creating real drama, they should allow her to fulfill her role as a troublemaker. When Aphrodite was present, there was no such thing as simple, idealized love. There was passionate desire and all of its attendant complications. In the *Iliad*, Paris, a Trojan, took Helen of Sparta off to Troy, provoking the Trojan War. Helen knew that she was wrong to be with Paris, and in fact became disillusioned with him, but she was compelled by Aphrodite to stay with him. Earlier, in a myth known as the Judgment of Paris, Aphrodite promised Paris that he would have the most beautiful woman in the world as his wife. When he took Helen with him to Troy he was fulfilling this prophecy, but Aphrodite also carried out her end of the bargain by commanding Helen to stay with Paris even after her affections had waned. Once again, those who fall under Aphrodite's influence are not allowed to escape a passionate dalliance without trouble.

Plato viewed Aphrodite as a representation of two kinds of love: a thoughtful, idealized kind of love and a more primal sexual love. Aphrodite was given many alternate names in her mythology, two of which are "Urania" and "Pandemos." Urania, which comes from her mythological beginning as the daughter of Uranus, means "heavenly" and was thought by Plato to represent a more idealized, pure love. "Pandemos" represents the other more physical kind of love and means roughly "common to all." At the *agora* in Athens, a kind of marketplace next to the Acropolis that served as a central gathering place, people would come together in assemblies called *agorai*. The name "Pandemos Aphrodite" represented her worship in these assemblies of common folk, and signified her connection with a more physical, earthly desire. Since Plato, Aphrodite has been more closely associated with this second kind of love. In essence, she has been more sexualized and more like we think of her today.

Aphrodite had as many as ten children, some of whom, such as Aeneas and Eros, are the subjects of poems and mythological tales of their own, and several of whom had wild, humorous, and in some cases tragic stories. In Hesiod's *Theogony*, Aphrodite had a daughter by Ares called Harmonia who, in later mythology, was given a necklace by Aphrodite's spurned husband Hephaestus as a wedding present, a gift that brought no end of trouble to those who subsequently stole it and used it as a bribe. Her union with Ares also produced two other children, Deimos and Phobos, gods of panic and fear. In the *Theogony*, Hesiod calls them "Terror and Dread," and says that they are responsible for wreaking havoc on the battlefield when frightened soldiers break ranks. Aphrodite's son Priapos, fathered by Dionysos, the god of wine, became a symbol of fertility in his own right. He was more a figure of fun than of serious worship, and his image—a little gnomish creature with a huge phallus—was often used by the Romans to decorate their gardens, where a statue of him was intended to be a kind of protector. As Aphrodite's son, he was an expression of the more purely lustful aspects of her role as the goddess of love and fertility, and so the Romans wrote short, humorous, and often sexually explicit poems in dedication to him. Another child, Hermaphroditos, said to have been fathered by the god Hermes, represented yet one more aspect of Aphrodite's embodiment of sexuality. In the *Metamorphoses*, Ovid tells of how a nymph called Salmacis fell in love with Hermaphroditos and, according to her wishes, was fused together with him so as to make one creature with both male and female parts, a kind of early representation of bisexuality.

Of all of Aphrodite's children, the one most familiar to today's readers is, of course, Eros—later called Cupid by the Romans. In the classical literature, it is not always clear that he is her son—the Greek poet Simonides makes him her child by Ares, but in Hesiod's *Theogony* he is actually present at Aphrodite's birth, and the Greek poet Sappho made him her child by Uranus, which would have made him a kind of half-brother to Aphrodite. Sometimes he is more like a companion to Aphrodite. He embodies many of the same qualities: love, both physical and idealized, and all its complications. He appears most often as a mischievous boy with wings and a bow and arrow; this image first appeared in Euripides' play *Medea*, an image now familiar to us from countless Valentine's Day cards. He embodies, perhaps even more starkly than Aphrodite, the idea that love must be accompanied by pain: to infuse a person with feelings of passion he uses a weapon to pierce his target's heart. One Roman story of Cupid and Aphrodite, by then known as Venus, shows us her two-sided nature as a goddess who can deliver both reward and punishment to those who love. Cupid falls in love with the beautiful Psyche but she disobeys him and he leaves her. Venus then makes Psyche endure a series of challenges while she searches for Cupid, wanting to reconcile with him. Cupid and Psyche are eventually reunited, but only after Psyche has emerged from Venus's trials to prove her love.

Aphrodite's purview was broad. She was worshiped and praised as the goddess of love, but her influence and the many qualities she embodied were far more nuanced and complex than the modern reader might guess. This tells us much about the ancient Greek understanding of love's many forms, and its delights along with its troubles. Through her many attendants and along the many branches of her mythology, Aphrodite acted as a sort of prism of these varied permutations of pleasure and desire. Poets, philosophers, and ordinary people found in her particular ideas and experiences of love, and they made her the incarnation of these. Aphrodite was enormously popular throughout the Greek world, and she was worshiped at temples dedicated to her throughout the mainland and the islands. Each of these cults was kept alive by common people and religious figures who devoted themselves to ensuring that the goddess was properly praised—and appeased—in thanks for her gifts to them.

APHRODITE'S SISTERS

One might regard Aphrodite and the other goddesses of the Olympian pantheon as an extended family of women meant to embody all of the qualities the ancient Greeks thought a woman might possess, given the right circumstances. The messy, changeable relationships among the gods and goddesses of the pantheon served to keep in check their power over humankind and over one another, and so Aphrodite's sisters, both literal—Athena and Artemis—and figurative—Hera, Hestia, and Demeter—were rivals, complements, and counterweights to Aphrodite's influence. Passionate love didn't hold much importance for these other goddesses, and they had little influence over humankind in this area. Whereas Aphrodite represented sexual desire, Athena, Artemis, and Hestia were all thought of as virgins; Hera, wife of Zeus, and Demeter, mother to the kidnapped Persephone, had other matters to contend with. Marriage, hearth, home, agriculture, fertility, all in stark contrast to Aphrodite's concerns as the goddess of love.

Hera is the wife of Zeus, and her primary role in Greek myths is that of a jealous wife, harassing Zeus's unwilling lovers or offspring. She is the goddess who defends the proprieties of marriage; she stays married and has no lovers herself. Hera's character emerges as rather severe, but perhaps her marital situation is sufficient cause.

We can imagine Hestia as the goddess of the hearth. She resides at home and we do not see her publicly. The last and least seen of Kronos's children, there are few myths about her. The Homeric hymn recounts that she was wooed by Poseidon and Apollo, but rejected both of them and swore an oath of eternal chastity, by touching Zeus's head. One may imagine Hestia as the daughter who never marries and who is chosen or chooses to live with and care for her parents as they become old and infirm. Hestia was more well known in Roman culture, where she was called Vesta. She embodies deep, individual reflection.

When one imagines Demeter, one must also imagine her adolescent daughter Persephone, who unwillingly became queen of the underworld. Demeter is the goddess of grain, who fructifies the fields of the earth that are plowed to support human life. A Demeter woman is often bountiful, matronly, and maternal—the original earth-mother. Her daughter, Persephone, is abducted by Hades into the underworld, where she reigns over the dead souls. A Persephone woman is the girl-woman who is easily taken; compliant and passive, her maiden powers render her eternally youthful.

A very definite, easy-to-spot archetype is that of Artemis, who is the Greek goddess of wild animals and vegetation, of chastity, virginal childbirth, and the hunt. (The Romans called her Diana.) Artemis delights in music and dancing in shadowy groves. Dancing maidens who represent nymphs are especially common as images of Artemis worship. One may find contemporary embodiments of Artemis in the National Park booth, explaining the topography of the surrounding land to all who enter the state park. The Artemis-only woman wears no makeup, is not concerned about the texture of her skin, and lets her unstyled hair go gray as she ages. She is at home in nature and not interested in displaying her beauty. In a classroom of young women, one can spot them by their shoes. They wear workout shoes, hiking shoes, maybe Birkenstocks—never strappy, colorful spike heels like their Aphrodite sisters. I saw an older Artemis woman on my walk the other day; she was tan, lean, wearing faded shorts and a shirt of no particular style, and her hiking books were old and purely utilitarian. Her gray hair was long and straggly, and she was alone except for the hounds who accompanied her. She could have been taking this same walk with the same hounds a thousand years ago, she was such an exact archetypal incarnation of this goddess. As the virgin huntress, Artemis belongs to the rural populace rather than the urban court. The hunt, the out-of-doors, areas remote and elevated, wild and untamed are her concern. Christine Downing warns that "Artemis also becomes the one who is hunted. Artemis represents the mystic, primitive identity of hunter and hunted."[11] Artemis is like Aphrodite in that Aphrodite hunts men and is hunted by men. For Artemis, as for Aphrodite, the absence of other modifying typologies may bring her doom.

The image of Athena most recognizable to today's readers comes from the mythology of her birth. She sprang, quite literally, from the head of her father, Zeus, after he swallowed Athena's mother to prevent her from having a child who might be more powerful than he. Athena emerged from her father in full battle gear, a warrior goddess right from the start. She was protectress of the city of Athens, and she was the goddess who guided men in war. Aphrodite, too, appeared on battlefields to stand by or rescue such heroes as her son Aeneas, but she was not a fighter dressed in a Greek soldier's armor, like Athena, whom Hesiod described in his *Theogony* as a "terrible rouser to battle and leader of armies."[12]

She was also the patroness of crafts such as weaving and metalworking, which, on the surface, may seem like an odd function to serve alongside her role as warrior goddess. Classics scholar Robert Towneley Parker shows that the two are in fact linked by Athena's virginity. Because Athena was regarded as a virgin, she could represent an activity usually associated with young girls, such as weaving or spinning, and she could also be viewed as less feminine because she hadn't given birth to a child. Her role as a warrior came directly out of this more masculine side of her nature. Parker also points out that not only was this goddess without children of her own, but she didn't have a mother. Athena was thought of as the offspring of Zeus alone. Childless and motherless, she did not possess the feminine instincts that might have caused her to want to pursue love or passion.[13] Aphrodite, too, did not necessarily have a mother, but she had many children, and her feminine qualities were her great strengths. In Athena's case, it was her lack of womanly qualities that made her the great warrior goddess who was worshipped as the patroness of Athens at her temple on the Acropolis.

LIVING EXAMPLES

I know a Hestia-type woman who has never married and does not venture far from home in her daily life. Her outgoing brother tends to almost all their worldly details and duties. She stays at home, sometimes for weeks at a time, painting. She wears no makeup at all, does not color her hair, and has no ideas, thoughts, or desires regarding style or being in style. She is not athletic at all, does not exercise, except for an occasional walk around the block with her brother. She drinks no alcohol, eats very little, and really does nothing to excess. She is a warm and kindly person. She is very reserved; she does not tell much about her own struggles and never gossips about others, unlike some of her other sisters. Just as in the ancient writings, there is little to tell about contemporary Hestias because they are at home and do not cause much trouble. The name Hestia means hearth, and she remains close to the hearth, the home. In the center of the hearth is the fire. The keeping of the flame must originally have been a religious, numinous experience. Without fire the world must have been cold, dark, and scary. Fire kept animals away and allowed for the cooking of food. Hestia types often have a religious aspect to their psyche; it is what is inside that is important to them. James Hillman has suggested that Hestia is the patron divinity of analysis itself.[14] She is the one who stays inside, literally, and stays connected to her inner world by recording her dreams and writing in her journal. While other types of women are out in the sun hiking or playing tennis or golf, Hestia is at home where it is safe and known. On the television series *Desperate Housewives*, Susan may be a Hestia type. She is introverted, likes to be at home, and is not so comfortable in the world. She is not ready and is shy about starting to date after her husband leaves her. She is an illustrator of children's books. Mary Alice, who dies in the first episode of the series, may also be a Hestia type, although we never learn very much about her. However, in that first episode we see her "quietly polishing the routine of her life."[15]

Jane Goodall and Amelia Earhart appear to be quintessential Artemis types. Goodall was asked to accompany the paleontologist Louis Leakey and his wife Mary on one of their numerous treks to the Serengeti Plain. At that time there were no tourists there, and it was very isolated and remote. They did monotonous, tedious work, digging for ancient fossils. In the ensuing years, her work caused her to risk plane crashes, malaria, hardships, rivers full of crocodiles, and the kidnapping of several of her students. Through it all, Jane Goodall survives.

Although Goodall stopped active field research in 1986 to focus on conservation, there has remained a mysterious connection between Goodall and Fifi, a chimpazee. Year after year, when Goodall returned to Gombe and entered the forest she knows so well, Fifi would appear, as if on cue—to the great delight of any accompanying film crew. Often Fifi would sit near Goodall, as she did so many times over the preceding forty-five years. Like old friends enjoying an overdue reunion, she and Goodall would sit still for a long time, and seem to commune in silence. Goodall's communion with animals is profound and demonstrates a deep connection with the goddess Artemis.

The ten-year-old Amelia Earhart saw her first plane at a state fair. Defying conventional feminine behavior, the young Earhart had climbed trees, "belly-slammed" her sled to start it downhill, and hunted rats with a rifle. She also kept a scrapbook of newspaper clippings about successful women in predominantly male-oriented fields, including film direction and production, law, advertising, management, and mechanical engineering. Earhart took her first flying lesson on January 3, 1921, and in six months managed to save enough money to buy her first plane. It was a secondhand, two-seater biplane painted bright yellow. Earhart named the plane "Canary," and used it to set her first women's record by rising to an altitude of 14,000 feet.

From then on, Earhart's life revolved around flying. She placed third at the Cleveland Women's Air Derby, later nicknamed the "Powder Puff Derby" by Will Rogers. As fate would have it, her life also began to include George Putnam. The two developed a friendship during preparation for the Atlantic crossing and were married February

7, 1931. Intent on retaining her independence, she referred to the marriage as a "partnership" with "dual control."

Earhart was not heard from again after her last flight, when she disappeared in the Pacific. The mystery surrounding Earhart's disappearance has long intrigued, excited, and haunted popular imagination. Over the years, many theories have evolved and several books have been written on the subject. Earhart had said, "Please know I am quite aware of the hazards. I want to do it because I want to do it. Women must try to do things as men have tried. When they fail, their failure must be but a challenge to others." Earhart is an amazing, lived example of having the Artemis archetype in her bones from childhood.

Sandra Day O'Connor is a stunning example of an Athena woman. She grew up on a cattle ranch in the southeastern Arizona town of Duncan. For schooling, she lived in El Paso with her maternal grandmother and attended the Radford School for girls and Stephen F. Austin High School, and then Stanford University, where she received her B.A. in economics in 1950. She continued at the Stanford Law School for her LL.B., serving on the *Stanford Law Review*, and graduated near the top of a class of 102, of which future Chief Justice William Rehnquist was valedictorian.

In spite of her accomplishments at law school, no law firm in California was willing to hire her as a lawyer, although one firm did offer her a position as a legal secretary. She therefore turned to public service, taking a position as Deputy County Attorney of San Mateo County, California, and then as a civilian attorney for Quartermaster Market Center, Frankfurt, Germany, from 1954 to 1957. From 1958 to 1960, she practiced law in the Maryvale area of the Phoenix metropolitan area and served as Assistant Attorney General of Arizona from 1965 to 1969. After that, she served in the Arizona State Senate and later as a judge of the Maricopa County Superior Court and the Arizona Court of Appeals. On July 7, 1981, President Reagan, who had pledged during the 1980 presidential campaign to appoint the first woman to the Supreme Court, nominated her as an Associate Justice of the Supreme Court.

Perhaps the ultimate Athena woman is Dr. Condoleezza Rice. Born November 14, 1954, in Birmingham, Alabama, Rice started learning French, music, figure skating, and ballet at age three. At age fifteen, she began classes with the goal of becoming a concert pianist. She earned her bachelor's degree in political science, cum laude and Phi Beta Kappa, from the University of Denver in 1974; her master's from the University of Notre Dame in 1975; and her Ph.D. from the Graduate School of International Studies at the University of Denver in 1981. After many years as teacher and administrator at Stanford University and work in U.S. government administration, she became the Assistant to the President for National Security Affairs, commonly referred to as the National Security Advisor, on January 22, 2001. Athena is an unmarried goddess. She is the shrewd companion of heroes and the goddess of heroic endeavor. She is the virgin patron of Athens. We do not know, of course, if Rice is a virgin, but she is unmarried and has never been married. She has never mentioned being on a date or being with a lover. She is the true daughter of the patriarchy; her companions are the heads of states.

Ultimate Demeter types have a particular sort of biography that belongs to these women alone. They are the ones you may read about in *People Magazine* who have adopted perhaps twenty children of many races, some with disabilities, and appear to have the resilience, warmth, and open arms for all the chaos that ensues. The shadow side of these women may be overweight issues, diabetes, heart problems, and no time for self-reflection. Often their husbands are viewed as mates to help with the children, and a vehicle to give them more children. They may have an overabundance of pets as well, and often these are rescued animals.

One example is a woman who was born and raised in Hilo, Hawaii. She and her husband have raised six children and have two grandchildren. Over the years, they have taken in about forty-eight children, teenagers, and adults who were in difficult situations and needed guidance and a place of peace and safety.

Another woman, at the age of ten, found herself advocating for children who were unable to speak up for themselves. As a teenager she realized that her life dream was to be married, have a family, and champion for children who were without families. At age twenty she married her sweetheart. At age twenty-two she gave birth to the first of her three children, and began fulfilling her dream to offer support for abused children by becoming a foster parent, four of which children she and her husband adopted. During the last thirty years she has addressed children's needs by advocating within the school districts for foster children as well as all children with disabilities. She teaches parenting classes and collaborates with schools and the community to address the issues of children involved in domestic violence. She is a popular and enthusiastic speaker on child advocacy and parenting skills.

Balancing Aphrodite

It is very important for an Aphrodite type to develop some relationship, psychologically, to the ways of being female represented by her sisters. The pure Aphrodite type is so poorly balanced that she may be almost a borderline personality. An example is Anna Nicole Smith; she was so exaggerated that it appeared she had no "sisters." I feel that the exaggerated Aphrodite women may be the ones who do not live very long. Another example is Marilyn Monroe, who became more and more reclusive as her years went by. Anna Nicole Smith also became reclusive, and was in bed a great deal the year before her death; the death of her son that year may have intensified this withdrawal. Sometimes drugs may add to the decline of these women when their youth starts to leave them and they are no longer so beautiful.

On the other hand, Angelina Jolie, certainly a beautiful Aphrodite, seems to have several "sisters" in her psyche: Demeter—thus all her children—and some Athena as well.

In the next two chapters we will see how analysis, therapy, and Jung's psychology have helped women to balance their Aphrodite qualities with the characteristics of her sisters.

Notes

[1] *The Homeric Hymns*, trans. Charles Boer, 2nd ed. (Dallas: Spring Publications, 1979), "The Hymn to Aphrodite," p. 73.

[2] *Works of Hesiod and the Homeric Hymns*, trans. Daryl Hine (Chicago: University of Chicago Press, 2005).

[3] Vinciane Pirenne-Delforge and André Motte, "Aphrodite," in *The Oxford Classical Dictionary*, 3rd rev. ed. (Oxford: Oxford University Press, 2003).

[4] *The Homeric Hymns*, trans. Boer, p. 69.

[5] *Works of Hesiod and the Homeric Hymns*, trans. Hine, p. 60.

[6] Theoi Project: Guide to Greek Mythology, online at www.theoi.com/ Olympios/Aphrodite (accessed January 2011).

[7] *The Homeric Hymns*, trans. Boer, "The Fifth Homeric Hymn."

[8] *Works of Hesiod and the Homeric Hymns*, trans. Hine.

[9] *Ibid.*

[10] *The Homeric Hymns*, trans. Boer, p. 80.

[11] Christine Downing, *The Goddess: Mythological Images of the Feminine* (New York: Continuum, 1996), p. 164.

[12] *Works of Hesiod and the Homeric Hymns*, trans. Hine, p. 84.

[13] Robert Christopher Towneley Parker, "Athena," in *The Oxford Classical Dictionary.*

[14] James Hillman in *Spring: A Journal of Archetype and Culture* (1998), p. 10.

[15] Janet Elizabeth McCabe and Kim Akass, *Desperate Housewives: Beyond the White Picket Fence* (New York: I. B. Tauris, 2006), p. 2.

Chapter 5

Understanding Aphrodite with the Help of Jung

> The dream is the small hidden door in the deepest and most intimate sanctum of the soul, which opens to that primeval cosmic night that was soul long before there was conscious ego and will be soul far beyond what a conscious ego could ever reach.[1]
>
> —C.G. Jung

C.G. Jung (1875–1961) is the founder of analytical psychology. He and Sigmund Freud worked closely for several years, but eventually split over their differing ideas on the nature of libido. Jung went on to develop his own theories, which he called "analytical psychology." Whereas Freud assumed a psychosexual explanation for human behavior, Jung perceived the primary motivating force to be religious in its foundation.

Jung is also known for his concept of the "collective unconscious" that is shared by all human minds. Deep within any human being's progress through the world—a journey that each of us tends to view as unique—are age-old, impersonal patterns of human experience that are as collectively conservative as they are individually creative. Both instinctual and spiritual in nature, the collective unconscious contains us and moves us forward in the half-light of our natural behavioral inclinations. At the same time, we are the recipients of its psychic images, by which our thoughts are organized and through which we can become significantly more conscious.

Jung's thinking as the founder of analytical psychology is seminal to this book, particularly his central concepts of individuation, archetypes, and the collective unconscious. Jung's panoramic view of the unconscious surpasses in its scope the old Freudian notion that the unconscious consists merely of repressed elements of the personal life experience. Jung, in contrast, urges us to consider that

> the unconscious . . . is the deposit of all human experience right back to its remotest beginnings. Not, indeed, a dead deposit, a sort of abandoned rubbish-heap, but a living system of reactions and aptitudes that determine the individual's life in invisible ways—all the more effective because invisible. It is also the source of the instincts. . . . From the living fountain of instinct flows everything that is creative; hence the unconscious is not merely conditioned by history, but is the very source of the creative impulse. It is like Nature herself—prodigiously conservative, and yet transcending her own historical conditions in her acts of creation.[2]

According to Jung, the archetype as an image of instinct is "a spiritual goal toward which the whole nature of man strives; it is the sea to which all rivers wind their way, the prize which the hero wrests from the fight with the dragon."[3]

The image of a hero fighting with a dragon—so familiar and fundamental to myths from many cultures—is an example of the psyche's form of storytelling. Myth, humankind's earliest literary creation, is an intricate blending of psychology and storytelling. Given this basic intersection between story and psychology, it is possible to explore Aphrodite in psychological terms: specifically, through Jung's elucidation of the psychological process of individuation, the collective unconscious, and the archetypes of which it is composed.

Jung's theory of archetypes, which he formulated in the early part of the twentieth century, provides a means of uniting the multitudes of images produced in myth, religion, all forms of art, dreams, fantasy—in short, all forms of human mental creativity—into broad categories that facilitate understanding of the entire image-making process. Jung called this tendency wherein many images constellate around certain core themes "an inherited mode of psychic functioning,"[4] and he believed that each of these themes represents a "universal, transcendental form-principle."[5] These "form-principles," or *archetypes*, are most easily recognized as the *generative forces* that give rise to the goddesses and gods of the world's mythologies. These same forces also *appear* in all realms of the human imagination; they are present in the arts as well as mythology, if one has the eyes to perceive their presence and the ears to hear their wisdom.

Applying a Jungian approach to the study of Aphrodite and her mythology requires us to understand the impact of the universal archetypes that are produced by the collective unconscious and are reflected in myths and narratives passed down through the ages. The basic assumption of this approach is that the individual human mind is interconnected with the collective psyche of humankind and may contain all or many of these archetypes from birth.

Jung divided the substrata of the human psyche into the personal and the collective unconscious. The former is the sum of individual experiences and repressed desires; the latter "contains the whole spiritual heritage of mankind's evolution, born anew in the brain structure of every individual."[6] The infant mind is not a *tabula rasa* (a "blank slate"), but is equipped with a specific a priori preparation for life, the common inheritance of the experiences of thousands of years. This area is more objective than the conscious mind because through it, by means of the archetypes, speaks elemental nature, un-swayed by the immediate environment affecting the other aspects of the mind.[7]

The archetype is a primordial pattern or form. It is not a stable element but is constantly changing.[8] It is the manifestation of the instinctive forces of the psyche, a dynamic and ever-creative impulse. An archetype may be infinitely developed and differentiated, and it has both a positive and a negative pole. One side points upward and is favorable or bright; another points downward, is unfavorable and in part chthonic or dark. Although Jung believed that there are as many archetypes as typical situations in life, he frequently referred to five in particular: the shadow, the anima, the wise old man, the mother image, and the child.

According to Jung, archetypes manifest themselves in various ways, frequently through rituals, dreams, and fantasy, and through mythology. Primitive tribal rites tend to confirm the theory of archetype by indicating a desire to confine and control a powerful instinct. Both dream and myth are also provinces of the archetype. A dream may be the most direct expression of the archetype, which is essentially an unconscious content.[9] Fantasy is another type of close contact with the oldest layers of the human mind. An individual may in fact identify with an archetype to the extent that the facts of the outer world are obscured and he or she experiences a drastic change of personality.[10]

On the ethnological level, archetypes appear as myths, though here they must necessarily have been modified by the individual consciousness of the artist or story. Myths reveal the nature of the human soul. They are symbolic representations of the drama of the unconscious become viable through projection into the events of nature. The gods and devils, magicians, werewolves, heroes, and villains of mythology are all dramatic and pictorial manifestations of nuclear elements within the deepest layers of the human psyche. This theory explains, too, why similarities in myths appear in cultures that developed independently. Jung stresses the fact that the powers that were once projected into gods and worshiped with sacrifices still play a vital role in our unconscious mind.[11] Mythology is the product of a strong inner compulsion. It is so basic, so inescapable, that given the destruction of civilization and tradition, it would be recreated *in toto* in the next generation. Jung states that the mystery of the creative process may be partially explained by an "unconscious animation of the archetype," which gradually develops into an image.

ANIMA, ANIMUS, AND THE CONIUNCTIO

Jung defines the anima archetype as an "omnipresent and ageless image, which corresponds to the deepest reality in a man."[12] The Aphrodite-woman is an "anima woman"—a woman who is the object of strong male projections and who herself has strong projections on others. This is the "not-I," the non-masculine element in man. Because of this archetype's power, Jung gives it the Latin name for soul and sometimes uses the two words interchangeably. Jung explains his concept of the anima archetype:

> Every man carries within him the eternal image of woman, not the image of this or that particular woman, but a definite feminine image. This image is fundamentally unconscious, an hereditary factor of primordial origin engraved in the living organic system of the man, an imprint or "archetype" of all the ancestral experiences of the female, a deposit, as it were, of all the impressions ever made by woman—in short, an inherited system of psychic

adaptation. . . . Since this image is unconscious, it is always
unconsciously projected upon the person of the beloved. . . .
I have called this image the "anima."[13]

I have seen this unconscious primordial aspect of the anima in men's
dreams and fantasies. Certain women seem born to carry this archetype,
and the Aphrodite type most often displays it. I remember seeing this
quality in my best friend's granddaughter when she was in preschool;
she is very pretty and fits a certain eternal type—which was apparent
even when she was only three or four years old. At the preschool, I
observed one little boy who was clearly "in love" with her, and their
antics mirrored those of adults. It was clear that she resonated with
the image that is engraved in his psyche. The young girls who become
prom queens and cheerleaders seem predominantly to be carriers of
this anima image, which men seek to locate in the outer world to
match their internal and eternal image. It is not only outer beauty,
but also a certain feminine essence that these women radiate and know
how to use. For better or worse, it is their fate to mirror the anima
that is embedded in the male psyche.

C.G. Jung writes: "The anima is often personified in myths and
fairy tales, also in dreams of regular people as a witch or a priestess—
women who have links with 'forces of darkness' and 'the spirit world,'
that is, the unconscious."[14] Even in old age, women born as anima
types gather male attention around them. Jung explains:

There are certain types of women who seem to be made by
nature to attract anima projections; indeed one could almost
speak of a definite "anima type." The so-called "sphinx-like"
character is an indispensable part of their equipment, also an
equivocalness, an intriguing elusiveness—not an indefinite blur
that offers nothing, but an indefiniteness that seems full of
promises, like the speaking silence of a Mona Lisa. A woman of
this kind is both old and young, mother and daughter, of more
than doubtful chastity, childlike, and yet endowed with a naive
cunning that is extremely disarming to men.[15]

The animus, meaning "mind" or "spirit," is the male aspect present
in the unconscious of women. Of these strongly magnetized
projections, Jung writes: "When animus and anima meet, the animus
draws his sword of power and the anima ejects her poison of illusion
and seduction. The outcome need not always be negative, since the
two are equally likely to fall in love."[16] The animus is the deposit, as

it were, of all women's ancestral experiences of men. Whereas the anima in a man functions as his soul, a woman's animus is more like an unconscious mind.[17] As a positive aspect of a woman's psyche, the animus is a bringer of light; it allows her to think clearly and creatively, and to differentiate and complete important tasks. In its negative aspects, the animus is opinionated and fixed in its ideas, which are often unoriginal. A woman I know who is an Aphrodite type and who has not developed her inner man, her animus, is remarkably opinionated and given to making collective remarks that are unsupported by her actual knowledge of the subject. She provides us with a good example of the way in which a woman's outer male companion may reflect her animus. A woman may be with a kindly man or a muscle-bound thug, a dropout or an artist, depending on her level of animus development. This particular woman's outer male companion has never been to college, is not able to earn a living, and is passive and allows himself to be bullied.

In depth psychology, romantic love is seen in terms of the projection of a man's inner woman, the anima, onto an outer woman, and of a woman's animus onto an outer man. This projection can stay pure, if it is not actualized. The man projects his own soul onto a real woman who is mostly unknown to him. He is projecting what is divine and mystical; the outer, real woman becomes an emblem of his soul. The anima and animus have been represented in many collective forms as Aphrodite, Athena, Helen of Troy, Mary, Sapientia, Beatrice, and Iseult—or as Hermes, Apollo, Hercules, Romeo, and Tristan.

A personal example of romantic love: I was in a plane flying from Madrid to Granada. The only other American on the plane was a handsome man who was seated next to me—and reading Jung! We had a passionate affair. I was sure that synchronicity had provided me with my divine partner. His grandfather was from Switzerland and had even known Jung. My lover lived in New York, and I lived in Los Angeles—which provided the elements of separation, longing, and burning desire. After passionate meetings in Colorado, the *coniunctio*— our conjunction—did not hold. The chemistry and the projection of my soul was as intense as I have ever felt. I suffered deeply.

While "falling in love" feels unique to the moment and to the individuals involved in the intimate relationship, it is essentially a collective experience. For the Aphrodite-identified woman who is naively persuaded by the uniqueness of her own life, the Rosarium pictures represent a potentially sobering and educative example of the male and female human being living out the ancient, ubiquitous, endlessly repeating and thus, utterly predictable pattern of emotion, fantasy, language, and behaviors associated with the experience of "falling in love." These pictures can provide a key to viewing her life more objectively.

The *coniunctio*—the conjunction of opposites—is an image of the goal of individuation—the psychological process that makes a human being an "individual," a unique, indivisible unit, a oneness. Individuation is a search for wholeness, for an integration of the personality. Individuation, as Jung perceives it, involves a realization of inner wholeness through the progressive and conscious experience of the psyche's contents, including the anima and animus. In 1932, Jung received a collection of alchemical treaties called the *Rosarium Philosophorum*, carrying illustrations from 1550. He was moved by these pictures, which led him to view alchemy as a projection of the alchemist's individuation process. The pictures depict stages in the relationship of a male and a female figure, a king and a queen. The coupling of a male–female pair—the *hieros gamos* or "holy wedding"— is a frequent image in world mythology of the ultimate fulfillment in individual development.

The first of these pictures portrays a fountain with a round basin (picture 1). "This is the so-called Mercurial Fountain, the fountain of Mercurius, and psychologically it would signify the foundation of the psyche prior to the birth of the ego."[18] The fountain basin is a smooth, unbroken round—there is no consciousness in the picture; it is pure psyche. This image of pure psyche brings to mind the stage when one is stuck in the roots of existence and is living in such a way that the "voice of God," of the Self, may not be heard. I am thinking of a former patient who slept with the television on all night long and

Figure 1.

smoked pot and drank a great deal—he seemed dulled, muted, and his soul was buried in matter. He existed in a uroboric, narcissistic state. He once told me a dream in which he was sucking his own penis. This man's psychology was similar to the Mercurial fountain—around and around with no outlet or goal. He seemed lost in the sea of unconsciousness, unable to awaken the creative power within him; there was little reflection. All is there in a mass of confusion, untampered-with and original.

In the second picture there is a king and queen; the queen stands on the moon, and the king stands on the sun. Their left hands are touching, their right hands are connected by two branches, and above them there is a dove. The unity depicted in the first picture has now been separated into two figures. Jung writes: "We must stress above all else that it depicts a human encounter where love plays the decisive part. The conventional dress of the pair suggests an equally conventional attitude in both of them. Convention still separates them and hides their natural reality, but the crucial

Figure 2.

contact of the left hands points to something 'sinister,' illegitimate, morganatic, emotional, and instinctive, i.e., the fatal touch of incest and its 'perverse' fascination."[19] When romantic relationships begin, it is the left-handed aspect of the relationship that activates the archetype of love. It is what we call "chemistry." The left hand has to do with the unconscious. The anima of the man and the animus of the woman have connected. What is below has connected as well as what is above. The fact that they have connected in the unconscious makes the contact deep—they have connected in the underworld. When a man and women meet and there is a right-hand connection only, the connection is then superficial, and there is not enough fascination to continue to the next phase.

The dove joining the couple is significant. Edward Edinger comments:

The dove has two major symbolic references: the Holy Ghost is one, and the dove of Aphrodite is the other. So symbolically these two different aspects are put together into one paradoxical image. . . . Psychologically this would mean that the beginning of the *coniunctio* is set off by an ardent desire—Aphrodite is the mother of desires—and this desire is at the same time an Annunciation of the Holy Ghost.[20]

There is a lesser *coniunctio* and a greater *coniunctio*. In the lesser *coniunctio*, the new attitude does not hold. This is often seen in intensely archetypal relationships that fall apart within six weeks, leaving the partners separated. Before they began the process, these people were filled with hope and desire. However, the *coniunctio* was unable to keep. The greater *coniunctio*, which is depicted in the last picture of the series, has to do with wisdom and love that are not contaminated with personal desirousness, manipulation, and power. The greater *coniunctio* is symbolic of the goal of individuation; however, individuation is a process, a journey—perhaps individuation is only finally achieved in death. Impulses toward the *coniunctio* are always at work in us, with the Self ever pulling us toward our destiny through passionate desire.

In picture three, the couple is now naked. Edinger writes: "As a process going on within a relationship, it would suggest that the two participants have shed their personas and are now approaching each other with what Jung calls 'the naked truth.'"[21] The partners are now beyond the flirting stage and have formed some commitment to the relationship. They are also more conscious, as their left hands are not touching but are connected by two flowering branches. This stage brings to mind the phase when one becomes relaxed with the other; the persona is down, makeup is removed, one feels somewhat natural being naked in front of the other.

Figure 3.

Picture four is the descent into the bath: the partners are sitting in what looks like a modern-day Jacuzzi. This is the descent into the water of the unconscious womb. In this stage, psychologically, there are often images of water: flooding, pools, lakes, ocean, baptism, a shower or bath, swimming, and drowning. It may be a regressive process; the weak ego loves this immersion, this surrender to blissful regression where there are no demands, a dissolving. It is an image of *participation mystique*, a term that describes a mystical connection wherein boundaries are thin and the subject has difficulty differentiating self from the other. At this stage, one might imagine that he or she has been joined to the other in a previous life; that the two separate, wandering souls have reunited at last. The merging in the mercurial fountain is experienced in different ways, depending on the level of ego development.

Figure 4.

In picture five, the couple is underwater. Jung writes: "The sea has closed over the king and queen, and they have gone back to the chaotic beginnings, the *massa confusa*."[22] The instinctual level is taking over. In this picture there is no consciousness, and the sun and moon are also submerged; the couple is in a fatal embrace. This is a truly passionate and yet unconscious union. At this stage, which is halfway through the pictures, the couple (in the outer world) may part, which may symbolize the lesser *coniunctio*. The love affair may then begin all over again with a new partner.

Figure 5.

In picture six, the couple is in a tomb. There are no longer two people, but one person with two heads. After the *coniunctio*, death often follows (an example is Tristan and Iseult). This is the stage of the night sea journey, the *nigredo*, the alchemical *mortificatio* stage. "*Mortificatio* is the most negative operation in alchemy. It has to do with darkness, defeat, torture, mutilation, death, and rotting. However, these dark images often lead over to highly positive ones—growth, resurrection, rebirth."[23] This stage often engages one's shadow, but out of the darkness may come the light. When one is in this stage,

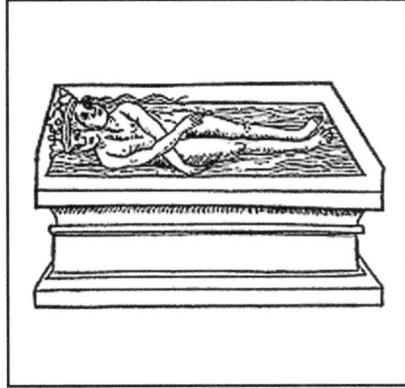

Figure 6.

one may experience intense suffering, despair, and defeat. Often the power-hungry ego must be cut down and humbled in order to kneel to the Self, to find the divine, to have a living relationship to one's soul. *Mortificatio* imagery brings to my mind a time when I was suffering and experiencing the dark night of the soul. My analyst at the time told me to be grateful, to thank God for this time of suffering because through it, one may then come into contact with the deep archetypal level of the psyche where God, or the transpersonal realm, may dwell.

An alchemical text says, "When you see your matter going black, rejoice; for that is the beginning of the work."[24]

Pictures six, seven, eight, and nine demonstrate the death of the soul, the separation of body and soul, and the reunion of body and soul.

In number seven, a little, tiny figure—a homunculus—is ascending from the tomb. The long period of depression and

Figure 7.

purification has begun. This picture shows a soul flying away: depression, like death, is a loss of soul. The partners have morphed into a single body with two heads; and like an empty shell, they lie in a tomb.

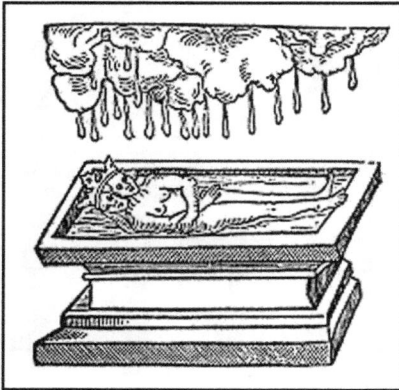

Figure 8.

In number eight, dew is dripping from a cloud over the lovers' united body, which is still in the coffin. The dew is referred to as *Gideon's dew*, which is descending from heaven. Jung says that this dew is referred to as the wonderful water that "purifies the body, and makes it ready to receive the soul; in other words, it brings about the *albedo*, the white state of innocence, which like the moon and a bride awaits the bridegroom."[25]

In the ninth figure, the tomb is open and within it lay the androgynous being toward whom the small homunculus silhouette descends. Breath returns. St. John of the Cross beautifully describes this stage when the soul is released and returns: "Two merging currents of the living spring—from these a third, no less astonishing in dark of night."[26]

Figure 9.

The last image in the series depicts a resurrection. The androgyne, the united king and queen, wearing two crowns, rises up victorious upon a quarter moon, while the tree of life grows nearby. We know so well in our bodies the power of the sexual call to union with another. This coming together of sexual opposites creates new life. It is that golden moment for which we long. In the union, the two are transformed, much energy is released, and the third element comes from it: the psychological child. The alchemists were concerned with the union of substances; by this means they hoped to attain the goal of their work: the production of the gold or a symbolic equivalent of it. The *coniunctio* experiences, the coming together of two unlike substances, is where the gold lies. They are the gold of the psyche, the golden moments that we long for and remember fondly.

Figure 10.

These ten pictures provide a map of the human psyche in regard to the stages of erotic love (as well as the analytic/therapeutic transference) and transformation. If one is aware of this important knowledge when in the throes of the drive toward *coniunctio*, one may not feel quite so alone, isolated, and lost. The result may not be as deadly. If one does not flee from relationship when things become dark, and then merely begin again with a new partner, one may ultimately obtain an inner marriage that leads toward individuation. The eternal may appear. Like alchemy, erotic love contains within itself the possibility of uniting two elements. In love the sexual and the spiritual may be united.

NOTES

[1] Jung, *Civilization In Transition*, *CW* 10, § 304.

[2] Jung, "The Structure of the Psyche," *CW* 8, § 339.

[3] Jung, "On the Nature of the Psyche," *CW* 8, § 415.

[4] Edward C. Whitmont, *The Symbolic Quest* (Princeton, NJ: Princeton University Press, 1969), p. 104.

[5] *Ibid.*, p. 75.

[6] Jung, *The Structure and Dynamics of the Psyche*, *CW* 8, § 342.

[7] Jung, *Symbols of Transformation*, *CW* 5, § 38.

[8] Jung, *The Archetypes and the Collective Unconscious*, *CW* 9/I, § 143.

⁹ *Ibid.*, § 6.

¹⁰ *Ibid.*, § 137.

¹¹ Jung, *Structure and Dynamics of the Psyche, CW* 8, § 728.

¹² Jung, *Aion, CW* 9/II, § 24.

¹³ Jung, *The Development of Personality, CW* 17, § 338.

¹⁴ C.G. Jung, *The Basic Writings of C.G. Jung* (New York: Modern Library, 1959), p. 541.

¹⁵ Jung, *The Development of Personality, CW* 17, § 339.

¹⁶ Jung, *Aion, CW* 9/II, § 30.

¹⁷ Daryl Sharp, *C.G. Jung Lexicon* (Toronto: Inner City, 1991), p. 23.

¹⁸ Edward F. Edinger, *The Mystery of the Coniunctio* (Toronto: Inner City, 1994), p. 40.

¹⁹ Jung, "Psychology of the Transference," *CW* 16, § 419.

²⁰ Edinger, *Mystery of the Coniunctio*, pp. 46-47.

²¹ *Ibid.*, p. 52.

²² Jung, "Psychology of the Transference," *CW* 16, § 457.

²³ Edward F. Edinger, *Anatomy of the Psyche* (La Salle, IL: Open Court, 1985), p. 148.

²⁴ Cited in *ibid.*, p. 165.

²⁵ Jung, *Mysterium Coniunctionis, CW* 14, § 155.

²⁶ St. John of the Cross, *The Poems of St. John of the Cross*, trans. John Frederick Nims (Chicago: University of Chicago Press, 1979), p. 43.

Chapter 6

Aphrodite in Analysis

A moment ago, and we were completely absorbed in the hectic, ephemeral life of the present; then, in the next moment, something very remote and strange flashes upon us, which directs our gaze to a different order of things. We turn away from the vast confusion of the present to glimpse the higher continuity of history. Suddenly we remember that on this spot where we now hasten to and fro about our business a similar scene of life and activity prevailed two thousand years ago in slightly different forms; similar passions moved mankind, and people were just as convinced as we are of the uniqueness of their lives.

—Jung, *Symbols of Transformation*, *CW* 5, § 1

Aphrodite is the most vulnerable of the goddesses—because she is the most focused on love relationships, in which impulse, loss, and suffering are built-in components. As the most resistant to transformation, with little capacity to relate to other archetypal qualities, she is the most doomed from birth. Artemis can go into the woods, Hestia can sit by the hearth and write in her journal, Athena can plan a battle or become a lawyer, and Hera can stay married and be a wife and partner. But Aphrodite is drawn solely to the next affair—it is very hard for her to focus on any other aspect of herself or the world at large. Indeed, an Aphrodite woman's world becomes animated by her fantasy as she falls into a state of "participation mystique," which is the experience of a mystical sense of connection or identity with another person. As noted earlier, the fall from such an inflated projection is a drastic one and typically plummets the woman into a deep despair. Aphrodites go through marriages and boyfriends, but as time moves on, they often end up alone or in an early grave.

Aphrodite is unable or unwilling to stick; she is not loyal. Thus she abandons, but is also abandoned. As David Lee Roth sings: "She loves you as you're leaving, but she will leave if you stay." How does such a woman change, if she can change—or is she doomed? I myself was fortunate, at age twelve, to have found literature, which saved my life the first time, and at twenty-four, to have found Jung, which saved my life the second time. The integration of some aspects of other goddesses, such as Athena, Hera, Artemis, and Hestia, in order to survive the shadow side of love, provides a partial answer to the question of possible change, but what is necessary to this integration is a feeling of humility. When one is cursed or blessed with the archetype of Aphrodite, one is inflated—large. But all glory is fleeting, and one must know when the party is over. The full answer may be *reflective* humility.

I am grateful that I came upon Jungian analysis and the wisdom of understanding dreams. When I told my first Jungian analyst a dream in response to his question, I knew I had come "home." My previous therapist, who was not Jungian, had never asked about dreams. To explain the impasse that we both knew we had reached, this therapist told me that I was like a brick wall, and he could not "get through" to me. What I learned in Jungian analysis is that when one tells a dream, one is immediately on the other side of the "brick wall."

The first dream I told my analyst was something like the *Sleeping Beauty* story, in which a rejected fairy curses the baby princess so that she and her kingdom fall into a deep sleep when she turns sixteen. When I began analysis, I was on the movie set and I was asleep, just as the cursed Sleeping Beauty slept. I was also powerless. As an extra and stand-in, I often did not know from one day to the next whether I would be working or not. While working on the set, all of us were continually on the phone, calling Central Casting, trying to get work for the following day. Thus I could never enjoy what I was doing or feel the least bit safe about where I was, because I was worried about the next day, year after year. And through it all, I was sure that if I met the right man, if the right prince would only kiss me, then I would be redeemed, like the princess in *Sleeping Beauty*. When my analyst told me the story of *Sleeping Beauty*—and how one day my animus, my inner man rather than some flesh-and-blood man, would kiss me (metaphorically) and redeem me, and that then I could pursue a course that had meaning to me—I was blown away by the archetypal hit. I felt hooked up to the eternal; it was an experience of a religious nature.

Putting words to such innate archetypal structures made sense to me. I went back to college within six months of beginning my analysis and eventually became a Jungian analyst and a mythologist. Not all patients who come for analysis get such an archetypal "hit." Some patients do not relate to the archetypal nature of the psyche and are impacted only by their subjective personal stories. I have interpreted early dreams, similar to the one I had, for patients who, for whatever reason, did not "get it." It is not meaningful to them that they may have dreamed of something from, say, the Bible or fairy tales, of which they had no conscious knowledge but which is in the collective unconscious. To others, however, such a realization is profoundly meaningful. The archetypal hit can be a saving grace for an Aphrodite woman who is submerged in her identification with the archetype. In my experience, professional as well as personal, it is the only kind of knowledge that has any sticking power for an Aphrodite and that may free her from the identification.

Another example of an archetypal dream hitting home comes from a new patient, an Aphrodite type. She had a recurring dream in which she is walking home from school, and an evil witch, following her, gains ground. The greenish-colored witch is a toothless hag who looms behind her. No matter how fast she walks, the witch follows closely, and the dreamer wakes up screaming. This hag is not unlike the left-out fairy in *Sleeping Beauty* who causes trouble in the background, who puts all to sleep—that is, eradicates any trace of inner drive toward consciousness. This shadow, this hag, must be humanized, or she will destroy and absorb the girl. Does the girl learn to make a conscious relationship to the hag, or does the hag get possession and power till there is no more girl? Fortunately, this patient was able to resonate to the deep archetypal layers that appeared in her dreams. Thus the fact that she has been so often depressed now has real meaning for her. Although my patient is young and pretty, often wearing a flower in her hair, she is frequently in the grip of this hideous, toothless, green-looking hag, an image of her depressive tendencies. But now she is conscious of this other side in her psyche and is able to turn and face it, to relate to it, instead of fleeing in terror.

At the beginning of a new love affair it is helpful to understand archetypal patterns. New love, positive or negative, acts on the psyche like a crisis. In the psyche of human beings there are archetypal engravings that are like a calendar for how we respond to crisis—a calendar that marks off archetypal time periods during which the "crisis" (whatever it may be) goes in one direction or the other. Let's consider the key blocks of time first and then consider the trajectory of a love affair in relation to them.

The first time period occurs in 72 hours—thus this is the amount of time that psychiatric hospitals hold patients, called the 72-hour hold. A hot, compelling attraction often ends in the first 72 hours. The second major time period is 40 days and nights—6 weeks, an extremely important time period in the psyche. Six weeks is the amount of time Noah's flood lasted, 40 days and nights; Moses was on the mountain for 40 days to receive the Tables of the Law; Christ was in the desert for 40 days and nights, and he was in the tomb 40 hours prior to his resurrection; after Christ was resurrected, he remained on earth 40 days before his ascension. This unit of time is sometimes used by contemporary police in regard to crisis intervention, and modern crisis intervention theory incorporates a 6-week time frame. It is healing in itself to know the ancient roots of this cycle. At the end of this time period, the grief has been worked through, or, in some cases, a maladaptive adjustment has been made that eventually leads to a psychosomatic or psychotic illness.

When patients are in a crisis—be it a new love affair (which acts on the psyche like a crisis), a move to a new house, or a new job—I often suggest that they note in their calendars when the first 6 weeks have passed. When the new union or resolution does not hold, it often falls apart at the fifth week and is over by the sixth week. After the sixth week, patients often report that they are on solid ground again. One returns to homeostasis—how one was before the crisis began. The lesser union is the love affair that ends before 40 days and 40 nights. Aphrodite "party girls" are well known for their preference for powerful but brief love affairs, during which the man often has already proposed marriage—and then things fall apart. For the party girl, there is no thrill to already gotten gain.

STEPHANIE: JOURNEY OF AN APHRODITE WOMAN

The following is a dream series of Stephanie, a fifty-one-year-old woman who is completely identified with Aphrodite to the very marrow of her now brittle bones. I have been working with her for thirteen years, and during that time she has become very interested in Jung. She reads many Jungian books and goes to analytical workshops in many parts of the country. Because of our work, she has developed other aspects of her personality, but Aphrodite she still is. This woman, who has been married four times, remembers one of her beautiful aunts telling her, "By the time you are finished, you will have been married more times than Elizabeth Taylor." When the aunt made this prophecy, Stephanie was only fourteen. She had the Venus vibe but did not feel particularly beautiful and was not that naturally beautiful—but some spark emanated from her, and she was asked to go steady on the first day of junior high school, not even knowing why she was being asked!

Stephanie had recently discovered that her fourth husband had been looking at pornography on the Internet. Another goddess was activated in Stephanie (and in other women with whom I have worked who have caught their husbands viewing porn on the Internet): Hera, the wife of Zeus. She is the wife and her domain is marriage. Harassing the lovers and offspring of Zeus, as the goddess who defends the proprieties of marriage, Hera has no lover herself. She does not like—in fact, she *loaths*—the gritty instinctual aspects of porn. Her domain is sex in the bedroom, not sex in the fields; she likes sex in the most conventional manner, unlike Aphrodite, who may be more open and experimental. When something invades her home—like these women's experience with Internet porn—she is extremely enraged.

And after Stephanie's discovery, she did become enraged—all the anger and abuse of her childhood came streaming into her. The negative aspects of her father, now the inner father, came out in uncontrollable anger that was destructive to her own psyche and certainly to any semblance of working this out in a human way with her husband. She could feel her hate in her cells. Stephanie suffered from a deep level of early disappointment in love, augmented by an archetypal fear of the patriarch.

At this time, she had the following dreams:

> Another woman and I cooked two cow heads in my kitchen in a boiling pot; they became brown and crispy, and then I somehow knew they were mad cows and I must throw them away. We put them in a bag and carried them to someone's house, maybe Anne's. Anne and her female friend did not want the cooked cow heads in their house, so the other woman and I put them in their trash cans.

> There was a man hiding in the shower behind a curtain when I came into a bedroom (not my bedroom, but where I was staying; I don't have a shower curtain in reality). I came into the bedroom and saw him crouching behind the curtain and woke up screaming loudly, "Daddy, Daddy!" at the top of my lungs. My husband woke me up.

> The Jungian scholar Sonu Shamdasani was in town; he was here at my house visiting, but not so much personally with me. There was another sort of man who had just woken up, walking down the hallway; it was morning. Sonu was sort of looking at my many books in my computer room. I thought maybe I should ask him if he would like to have dinner here or go for a walk with me around the neighborhood.

Stephanie's associations were that she felt like a crazy, mad cow with all her anger toward her husband as well as herself; she could feel the hatred in her own heart. The crouching man and the calling of "Daddy, Daddy!" brought to Stephanie's mind the many dreams she has had during her lifetime of this nature, waking up screaming. A male stranger tries to break in, and she wakes up in terror. "I suppose I called for Daddy because he was my salvation as a child, but he was also abusive; he tried to hit me over the head on one occasion with his golf club. No one else could help but my daddy, even with his bad, terrible parts." Shamdasani is someone she greatly admires.

One may say that Stephanie's husband deserved her rage (in her view) for breaking his vows and injuring the container of the marriage, but there are more human ways of reconciling painful things than giving in to rage. Stephanie's rage went on for weeks, and she felt as though she were filled with excrement. Toni Morrison writes:

> Before I was reduced to singsong, I saw all kinds of mating. Most are two-night stands trying to last a season. Some, the riptide ones, claim exclusive right to the real name, even though everybody drowns in its wake. People with no imagination feed

it with sex—the clown of love. They don't know the real kinds, the better kinds, where losses are cut and everybody benefits. It takes a certain intelligence to love like that—softly, without props. But the world is such a showpiece, maybe that's why folks try to outdo it, put everything they feel onstage just to prove they can think up things too: handsome scary things like fights to the death, adultery, setting sheets afire. They fail, of course. The world outdoes them every time.[2]

The "mad cow" head is a bovine state of archaic and primitive aspects of the psyche, coming from deep in the collective unconscious. Bovine spongiform encephalopathy (BSE), commonly known as mad cow disease, is a fatal, neurodegenerative disease in cattle that causes a spongy degeneration in the brain and spinal cord—the microscopic appearance of "holes" in the brain, degeneration of physical and mental abilities, and ultimately death. Stephanie felt like she had holes in her brain; cruel things she did not mean came flying out of her brain and out of her mouth. In the dream, Stephanie is trying to cook the cows' heads, making them crisp and thus drying them out, attempting to perform an alchemical process on them. In alchemy, what is too wet must be made dry; what is too dry must be made wet.

Someone with too much "Aphrodite fluid" must dry out a bit. If a patient cries all the time in session, it is important at some point that the moisture, the torrent of tears, not flow so heavily. On the other hand, if a patient never cries, one hopes that tears and feelings will come forth. In analysis, one looks for the other side. If there is too much darkness, one hopes some light will come; if someone's attitude is too light, too overly spirit-bound, one must bring in some darkness, some weight.

The mad cow heads are corrupt and contaminated; making them crispy takes the destructive juice out of them. At an instinctual level, my patient had become very disturbed. The women go off to try to cook the "matter." The dreamer then tries to give it to "Anne," who in reality is a therapist who sees dreams and situations in only a personalistic way. Sex addiction, however, is not only a personal therapeutic issue—sex addiction, which may not even be the case with Stephanie's husband (but to Stephanie it was a hideous infidelity, thus her dream and her reaction), is a collective issue like alcoholism, and needs a collective, not simply a personal, container—so the cow heads are put in the trash to be picked up by the city, the *polis*: this is the proper antidote.

The appearance of dream imagery in duplicate pairs, like our two cow heads, is generally indicative of new and provocative contents emerging from the unconscious. The cow is a universal symbol of the Great Mother, but things take a retrograde turn here toward the darker organic realm over which she presides. The cooking and drying of the cow heads may reflect the dreamer's dismay with her husband's interest in pornography as contrary to the Mother's right order of things as well as a personal insult. The heads thus are initially like biohazard waste infecting the individual, but also undergoing a purposeful process that may move the dreamer and her husband from their first emotional responses toward a more open and objective way of assessing sex, the relationship, and themselves.

Interestingly, Stephanie's story, and all the stories I currently hear about men and porn, have to do with the Internet—the spidery web of the whole world. What could be more collective and less personal? So, the recipe: cook the cow heads in the pot until crispy, take out the moisture, the craziness, the too much wetness, and dispose of them. Like alcoholism, pornography needs a religious attitude to cure it, not just a personal attitude. A larger consciousness is required. In AA meetings one does not dispose of one's problem alone; it is taken to a meeting—in the city, in the *polis*, among others in a worldwide collective—to deal with the issue. The ideal would be for Stephanie and her husband to participate in a psychological "rinse cycle" and dispose of the tainted two-headed beast.

As to the aspect of the dream with Sonu Shamdasani: he is perceived as highly Apollonian, quiet and reflective. It took him thirteen years to edit Jung's *Red Book*, also known as *Liber Novus*. He is an amazingly positive animus figure in Stephanie's dream, and he appears in her computer room where she does her intellectual work, which is somewhat new to her—she works at being a writer. During her life she has had very negative inner men appear, with few redeeming aspects, but over the years these men in dreams have developed and are not just scary monsters trying to break into Stephanie's home to harm her. Perhaps the crouching man is behind the shower curtain because the possibility of a baptism is taking place: a rain shower, refreshing and cleansing. In many films, one knows that redemption is near when the rain falls, or when a hero or heroine is bathing in some form. And now Shamdasani appears, the editor of the *Red Book*. Jung's *Red Book* describes his conscious descent into the unconscious; the book holds his madness and his journey alone in a fearful inner desert, his journey to the underworld and his profound insights. It was a mystery surrounding the recovery of his soul.

Of course for an Aphrodite woman like Stephanie there is no greater infraction than for her mate to be drawn to other women. "Mirror, mirror, on the wall, who is the fairest one of all?" Instead of killing Snow White, my patient wanted to kill her husband—or the anima in him that was more beautiful and much more alluring than Stephanie herself.

After working with me for some weeks on the "mad cow" dream, Stephanie had the following dreams:

> I was in the lobby of a movie, and I saw Beverly. She wore no makeup, and I almost did not recognize her. I did not wear any makeup either. We greeted each other, and she said that I looked great.

> I was at a place with a big pool of some type. I wanted to dive in from high up, but I did not. But I did dive in, after some time, at a medium place. I dove a number of times.

> I saw from a distance into the pope's bedroom. Before this he was outside in his vestments, leading a ceremony as he does in Rome. I saw that he was asleep in this room, on his bed in normal clothes, and then I saw that he'd died.

Beverly is a friend of Stephanie's who is very appearance-oriented and has had a number of cosmetic procedures. She is someone who would be hard pressed to go out of the house without makeup and perfectly dressed hair. As a younger person, Stephanie was the one to always dive off the high board, to be the best diver; as a two-year-old child she would dive off the high tower when she went to a local resort with her parents, and her father would be there as she dove into the water, to help her swim to the edge of the pool. For Stephanie, who is not Catholic, the pope is a powerful patriarch; Stephanie related how many popes throughout history have hidden the abuse of little children by priests.

In the dream, Beverly and Stephanie connect with each other in a new way. Each is bare of makeup—they do not have on their protective personas. They are more human and vulnerable. In the next dreams Stephanie does not have to dive from the high tower anymore; she can take the middle way, the medium height. She does not have to be with her father, but can manage the water on her own. Anyone can dive into the water, which is generally symbolic of the unconscious—but the goal is to dive in and recover, to be able to go into, and also get out of, the water.

The pope may be symbolic of the executive function in the psyche; in Stephanie's dream, he is now dead.[3] Thus the former powerful king or pope in Stephanie's psyche is dead, and a younger, more vital animus image appears in the form of Sonu Shamdasani. The animus is not only a personification of masculine qualities, but he also carries the ideas, the hopes, the wishes, and fears women have had about men throughout the ages.

A few weeks later, Stephanie dreamed that she was in a dress store, a fancy one, with her friend Judi, and that they both bought expensive tops. "Mine was pink, hers gold with jewels. I decided to take mine back—maybe there was something wrong with it—a little thread loose or something. I then went back to the store and bought a dress, nothing like what I really wear. It was an ankle-length dress with a built-in waist, and form fitting, but not sexy form fitting—more like a shirtwaist style on top, maybe with a prim little white collar, and sleeveless, with stripes. I later wanted to take it back."

In this dream, Stephanie is with her friend Judi, who is a member of the Aphrodite species—you can spot them like spotting species of birds. Judi is an older Aphrodite woman who also has been married a number of times, is married currently, and even though she is in her sixties, she has a lover who lives six thousand miles away with whom she rendezvous every few months and with whom she shares great passion and romance. Judi in reality is all jewels and sparkles. In the dream, Stephanie takes back her pink "Eros" top—something was loose or damaged about it—and she buys a conservative, ankle-length dress, ankle-length in a kind of schoolteacher style with a little puritan collar. So her psyche is trying on a different style, but it does not yet really work, a style with different stripes—but an animal never changes its stripes, so the dream is trying to work it out, as dreams do in order to compensate for one's conscious attitude. Samuels writes, "Compensation means balancing, adjusting, supplementing. [Jung] regarded the compensatory activity of the unconscious as balancing any tendency towards one-sidedness on the part of consciousness."[4] Stephanie could use a change of style—although at age fifty-one, she still dressed like a teenage rock star, and she still got away with it. But her dream suggested it was time to reconsider.

It is clear from the suggestions in Stephanie's dreams that her psyche wants to propose other ways of being than submitting to total control by the Aphrodite nature. The pure rage at her husband's infidelity (in her view), characteristic of an Aphrodite attitude, might be replaced by a willingness to work with her husband in seeking to free him from his interest in pornography—or joining him. The fear of a threatening masculine, figured in images of men who want to attack her or control her (the pope, the patriarchy), may be replaced by the admiration of another kind of masculine, reflective and related, imaged by Shamdasani and present in her own being, as evidenced in her new involvement in writing. The diving from the middle position, easily in and out of the water, reflects her increase in consciousness, and the new dress suggests that she is no longer helplessly compelled to conform to Aphrodite-style dressing; she has a choice.

CINDY: SEARCHING FOR APHRODITE

Other women come to me with a missing or damaged Aphrodite aspect, and they want to develop it. Many of them are women around thirty-something years old who want to meet a guy, get married, etc., so they go on the Internet. They may be nice looking, but Aphrodite does not live inside of them, and they do not attract men. So, we talk about things such as what to wear, how high the high heels, what kind of makeup, and so on. This sounds superficial, but the work goes along with what comes out of dreams and fears and stories of childhood.

This point is illustrated in Cindy's story. Her parents divorced when she was two, and her mother abandoned her when she went off with another man. This double whammy of abandonment is deep inside of Cindy. Her mother's abandonment of Cindy resulted in a core feeling of rejection, which then became a host environment for profound feelings of shame and humiliation. Once these feelings fully descended upon Cindy, she worried about and identified with homelessness, as further evidenced by images of homeless people in her dreams. Beneath her quiet but friendly persona resided dark, chaotic feelings of being defective and unlovable. The mirror for her young life, for her existence, was her mother. Then her mother left her with another mirror, her father, and she started to adapt to it. She began to become the reflection of her father, and then Lawrence.

Cindy had had a significant and powerful ten-year relationship with a young man named Lawrence. Her first sexual experience occurred with Lawrence. Her feelings about this relationship were alive in her heart and in her dreams. She had firmly believed that she and Lawrence would be married, and she was devastated when she began to sense that he had stopped loving her. She tried to hold on to him by behaving as if everything were just as it had been, and she never revealed her underlying fear of not feeling loved. As a result of the breakup with Lawrence, her world fell apart and her sexual nature receded behind the safety of concealment.

She told me about a man with whom she had had a weekend affair. A week after their encounter he had sent her some yellow roses (which represent friendship) and had never called her again. She cried, saying that it was time for her to look at her problems with men. Although heartbroken, she began to worry about the larger pattern in her relationships. She stated that she liked her job and friends; however, no one loved or cherished her and, for that loss, she suffered. The romantic side of her had been wounded in a profound way. She had never really found a deep love again. The sexy, hot side of her could not again go through such a profound loss.

In the course of our work together, Cindy had this dream:

> I am outside on the beach, and there are waves breaking on both sides of me, the left and right—or front and back, depending on which way I am standing—on this strip of sand. The water is crystal clear, turquoise, Caribbean perfect. I am there with a man and a woman (both unknown to me). I think there is also a truck on the sand, and a log that is standing upright and maybe sometimes lying down so that I could hide behind it, but I am very wary of it, knowing that one should not turn one's back on large driftwood at the beach, because if a wave catches the wood, the wood might be hurled into you or over you.

> I am also watching the waves. Swimming in the waves is a whole flock of rabbits. They are really huge rabbits, and as they go over the swells in the water, their white fluffy tails flash

behind them and their ears stand up above the water. They are incredibly amusing and adorable to watch. I must get a picture of them, so I try to find my camera, even though I am worried about getting it wet.

Lauren comes out of the bedroom finally. She has changed into an Asian woman, dressed in a hot-orange pantsuit, very mod. I go to the window and look out and see all these men, lots of beautiful ones, ready for the festivities. Lots of them have their shirts off and are really tan. They look great, but I think to myself that probably most of them are gay.

Cindy had these thoughts about the dream: "The log reminds me of something I learned as a kid—not to turn my back on the ocean. The log is something to keep my eye on, but also something to cling to. . . . The beach seemed the perfect place for a summer romance—a Judy Bloom book where the ugly duckling meets a boy at the beach. I never met anyone. I felt happy and sad then. The gay men make me feel incompetent. If I knew the recipe, I would fix it. . . . It's not fair that fate does not cross my path with a psyche that fits with mine. I would be mad if Lawrence was my only great love and it was over by age twenty-four. I was nervous then and I'm nervous now. Lawrence and I both worked with deprived children in high school. Since high school we spent every day together. The relationship with Lawrence was cerebral and also a spiritual connection. Great sex, but more. We were very drawn to one another, spent so much time together. It hurt me so badly when he didn't love me anymore. I could still easily cry when I talk about him. When we broke up, I didn't know if I could do it—be in life without him." This lament brings to mind the words of Plato:

> Man's original body having been thus cut in two, each half yearned for the half from which it had been severed. When they met they threw their arms around one another and embraced, in their longing to grow together again, and they perished of hunger and general neglect of their concerns, because they would not do anything apart.[5]

I said to Cindy that her description of her breakup with Lawrence and how she felt sounded like when she was little and attached to her mother, an attachment that was repeated in her profound attachment to Lawrence. The dream setting suggested that Cindy was opening to an experience of the unconscious. Her mention of the "waves breaking on both sides of me . . . front and back" seemed to imply a realization that the attitude one takes toward the unconscious might be important. That the water is crystal clear suggested an increasing clarity toward unconscious processes. In the midst of this scene, there was a log that could either provide a hiding place, something to cling to, or in some way endanger her. Perhaps the log suggested a psychic complex of which she was just becoming aware. Since there was an unknown man and woman there too, it suggested that this complex might have to do with her ambivalent attitude toward sexuality.

This suggestion of sexuality was further borne out by the image of rabbits, presented in an almost surrealistic manner, yet "incredibly amusing and adorable to watch." The rabbits bring to mind the saying "fuck like a bunny." Rabbits are a universal symbol of fecundity. Cindy's attempt to get a picture of this scene led to anxiety about the camera getting wet. "Getting wet" also suggested her fear of getting close to sexuality. With a wet camera the recorded memory of this image could be washed away, suggesting her ambivalence.

Lauren (the woman in the dream in the orange pantsuit) was a friend of Cindy's whose relationship with her lover had ended. However, she had quickly met someone new and was now married. In the dream, Lauren was transformed into an Asian woman in a "hot-orange pantsuit." The dream suggested that Lauren was a shadow figure who was capable of a new relationship and dressed in a way Cindy did not dress—flamboyant and sexual. Lauren was now Asian; Cindy felt that Asians had a sense of entitlement that she did not have. Her self-deprecating attitude toward life was now being transformed in the figure of Lauren, who is now perceived as Asian.

The gay men had to do with Cindy's experience on an AIDS walk. She had been hoping to meet a new boyfriend; however, most of the men were gay. Perhaps one safe way of dealing with her sexuality, as in the dream, was to imagine that the appealing men she saw were gay.

Each section of the dream ended with a negative, a "yes—but," that perhaps revealed Cindy's underlying depression. I believed that the dream was hinting, however ambivalently, that Cindy's psyche was getting ready for a new relationship. Sure enough, a month after being accepted into a fine arts master's program, Cindy met a new man, Warren, who had a powerful effect upon her. She told me: "I used to manipulate myself to be whatever the other person needed. If he was a marathon runner, I would then become one. It's so painful if it doesn't work out. I will feel so rejected letting someone in. It's so new to me. I am making progress in keeping hold of who I am with Warren. I used to try to hide myself. I feel cautious. I don't want to throw myself away."

Cindy's is the story of a woman whose connection to sexuality, her sense of belonging, safety, and worthiness was broken as a little child with the abandonment by her mother, and repeated with Lawrence. In order for Cindy to experience Aphrodite again, these early experiences must be sorted out and deeply felt. Cindy's mother was an Aphrodite type who was stabbed by Eros and fled from Cindy and Cindy's father. Lawrence was stabbed by Eros and fled from Cindy. Cindy herself was not born an Aphrodite type; she is more a sister to Artemis and Athena. Delving deeply into the personal, her unique history, and into the collective aspects of her psyche would be necessary before Cindy will feel whole enough to trust love again—to feel the beauty and lure of Aphrodite, the prick of Eros, the blood and vitality of love.

APHRODITES AND THEIR FATHERS

In my analytic practice, many of the Aphrodite types I have worked with were "father's daughters"—heavily identified with and in thrall to a certain form of the masculine principle. One of these women who was very close to her father, although not concretely incestuous (psychological incest may be just as powerful as actual incest), shared many intimacies with him as a young and grown woman. In one of her dreams, after we had worked together for three years, she was in a beautiful park with her great-grandmother. In the dream, they were meeting each other for the first time, and they held each other with affection. My patient in reality did not know her great-grandmother; thus it is the great archetypal mother whom she embraced, and whom she so dearly needs to help balance out her overvaluation of the masculine principle. In reality, her great-grandmother was said to be an independent cattle rancher who raised four children and constructed her own ranch. I used to think of this beautiful patient as a "party girl," since being a party girl was her main interest—finding guys, falling in love with them, and then moving on to the next one. The image of her great-grandmother is just what she needs—far away from the glitter of parties and new boyfriends and the perfect alternative image for a dependent female in service to the masculine. Her great-grandmother carried her own healthy masculine, and as a dream image she forecasts this patient's emerging healthy animus. Such an animus is essential if a father's daughter is to stand on her own, outside of the shadow of patriarchal approval or disapproval.

Another Aphrodite patient, Betty, who is in her late sixties, goes to Tuscany every year. She recently told me, "I think this is my last time in this town, as the guys are too aggressive and jealous of each other and emotional; they are always trying to be my lover. Here you actually have to fight off the guys, and that is not so much fun now that I have other interests to fall back on, such as reading, ballroom dancing, and hiking. Before our work, only the guys gave me meaning." Since junior high school Betty has been called a "man magnet." She really did not know why she was so picked out of the crowd by boys and men. To this day Betty has a powerful, compelling relationship with her father. Although they did not have sex, she shared a bed with him even as a young and grown woman when they were on vacations together.

The father is a young girl's first love and the template for all future loves, be it a positive or a negative template. For an Aphrodite girl, winning the eye of the father is perhaps more important, or more urgent, than for young girls with other goddess influences. Turning the father's head is central, is absolutely essential, to the young Aphrodite, whose tender core is already orienting powerfully toward fulfilling the drive to attract, to enchant.

Not all Aphrodite women have close positive connections with their fathers; some suffer from the reverse—negative and possibly abusive connections. One such patient told me the following dream: "My house is filled with probably a hundred pigs. They are on their stomachs, partly encased in cement, but they are alive." My patient's father was an alcoholic who drank up his paycheck, often leaving the family without money to buy food. He terrorized the family and was brutal to his girls. My patient's husband is not brutal physically, but she is afraid of him and "walks on eggshells." He gobbles up all of their money on various stock and bond market schemes and other investment deals, so that even though he makes a large salary, they are in debt. She really believes she should honor and obey. She is a churchgoing Catholic, so God the Father and his priests are important in her life; it is hard for her not to obey something a priest might preach or say to her.

We have been working together for over ten years, and it is clear that what she must do is to love and obey herself and the Self within her, rather than the masculine as it appears in her husband and the Catholic patriarchy. My patient cannot change her husband—she has tried it all: dialogue, therapy, and on and on. He most likely will not change and will keep spending all of their money—but she can change and she has changed.

Pigs are a fertility symbol; we think of a mother pig and her piglets. It is important for my patient to realize that these pigs are stuck in cement. I feel the dream was really trying to convey, in "concrete" terms, the pig-like nature of her father–daughter–husband relationship. Before her marriage she had an Aphrodite streak; men were very attracted to her glowing ways, her revealing outfits and sparkly jewelry. It is all gone now—covered over by gray, granular cement! If she dresses in a compelling manner, her husband makes her feel guilty and sluttish. She needs to realize what her soul calls out for, not what her husband wants her to be. She was not born to be his servant but to serve her own soul. The house is often a symbol of one's psyche, and in this case, things look pretty immovable. How to get those pigs out of there, I do not know; perhaps one has to move in the outer world or move to a new psychic space in the inner world. It is important for this patient to know that she can't move the pig-like aspect of her husband, but she herself can change. It is time for her to live the symbolic life, to experience freedom, and to *not* be cast in cement in the concrete world of all the details she has to take care of because of her husband's many "deals." In this patient, Aphrodite and Demeter, whom she needs to propagate her own soul and to care properly for her children, are stuck! The domestic pig indicates fertility; this woman's psychological fertility is encased in cement—held immovable by the masculine.

Another sexy-looking patient, who has had many relationships and draws men easily, as a young girl was very attached to her well-educated and religious father. He was stern, and sometimes violent. She relates this dream:

> I am at a dinner in an old-English-style room. There is a vicar at the head of the table. I am there with my boyfriend. There is a small round of butter on the table, about the size provided for two people. The round has a hole in the center, and it is frozen hard; it is so hard that it can't be used.

In reality, this patient likes butter; butter is what makes bread yummy. Butter is a soft, yellowish or whitish emulsion of butterfat, water, air, and sometimes salt, churned from milk or cream and processed for use. In antiquity, butter was used for fuel in lamps, as a substitute for oil, to light the way. In India, butter, called *ghee*, has long been a symbol of purity and has been used as an offering to the gods—especially to Agni, the Hindu god of fire—for more than 3,000 years. And it is used for ceremonial purposes such as fueling holy lamps and funeral pyres. Up to recent times, butter was also used for medicinal purposes; I remember as a child my mother putting butter on my arm when I burned myself. The meaning and symbolism of butter go on and on.

But in this young woman's dream, the butter cannot be used. There is no "butter up" between herself and her lover, no oil to lubricate their love. And at the head of the table, in the dominant position, is the vicar, a clergyman appointed to act as priest of a parish—so an aspect of the God the Father is at the head of the table. There is no lubrication for love, for romance, for the couple when Father is running the show. If the butter were soft, it could be spread and digested by the couple.

KORY: DEATH, DESPAIR, AND PHALLIC ENERGY

Kory's Aphrodite connection was almost quashed early on by trauma. However, she is very interested in men—styling her long tresses, dressing fashionably, being attractive and standing out. There is a part of her that is a natural Aphrodite type.

Kory lost both her parents when she was three, and was brought up by her aunt, a cruel woman similar to the evil stepmother in Cinderella. Her aunt turned a cold shoulder to Kory's profound early loss, and as Kory grew older, she attempted to squash Kory's budding

sexuality. As Kory recovered her feelings about those early years of loss
and harshness, changes began to emerge. At the beginning of our third
year of work, Kory had a dream that had a great impact upon both of
us. It made visible an aspect of her psyche that shifted our work to a
new level. It was a dream that I frequently felt and remembered when
I was in the room with her. The dream brought both Kory and me
closer to her underlying depression. Through the dream we were both
exposed to the seriousness of her despair.

> I am running around an almost empty landscape at night; all
> there is to see is a gas station with one light on. I am in this sort
> of agony, trying to scream "Help me, help me," but I can't get
> the sounds out at first, and then I do, but there is no one to
> hear. I think all I want is to tell whomever I can tell that I am
> afraid, afraid maybe of continuing to live. Finally, I rally a few
> people, and I am carrying on about how I can't bear to go on
> living, it's just too terrible.
>
> We are sitting in a sort of square. Although there are more
> people, my friend Nick is the only one I know. I think he is
> holding my hand.
>
> I am watching an anguished young man talk, but he is me. He
> breaks down and says, "No, I can't go on living, you must
> understand—if my heart simply stopped beating, it would be
> the best thing."
>
> Then there is a noise and we pause. I think to myself, it is someone
> with a gun coming to kill us all, and I realize I am scared to death.
> But then there is another pause and we realize that the sound is
> not of a person but the sound of an earthquake approaching.
> That's when I woke up, with a start and a terror, and I was scared
> we were having an earthquake here at three A.M.

Kory had a rich set of associations to this powerful dream with
its several segments. She noted: "Four people are in a square in a
barren area, like highway I-5 at night. I am in agony; I scream to
people but there is no one to hear. I didn't think they could hear
me. Nick in the dream is a friend who does not have his act together.
He is a glassblower, but he does not make much money and has
not gotten on with his life.

"The man is young, like me (the second man). He is heartbreaking
because he seems so good—like a Jesus sort of person—Jesus is so

tolerant and understanding. The young man is the saddest fellow in the world. He is hopeless and wants to die; his heart is hurting. He has been there since I was born. He is like a child who was born and then his parents died. He has always been there."

I asked Kory to name this young man, and she said his name was Jerome. I felt that this was a breakthrough dream because Kory's psyche could now reveal her despair; she was exposed to the seriousness of her own life. She was "running around in an almost empty landscape," which suggested a manic feeling and a sense of having no inner resources; she was bereft and depressed. There was a gas station; gas is a volatile mixture of flammable liquid and it is used as fuel for internal combustion and illumination. Gas is life-giving and the opposite of the "ashes of mourning." I viewed the gas, the light, and the square as hopeful symbols in this dream image of Kory's almost barren inner landscape. Kory needed the tremendous energy of gas to ignite her. However, gas by itself is nothing; what transforms gas into fuel is some kind of spark. She was not able to use the gas in the dream. The square, though, was an image of wholeness, an image of possible future potential becoming manifest.

That there was no one to hear her screams would refer to her aunt's cold shoulder and may also have been an aspect of the transference. I wondered if I had been so aligned with helping her restore her outer life that I had failed to hear her deep despair. The figure of Nick suggested an inadequate, unsuccessful, antihero image (he was also in her initial dream). That he was holding her hand brought to my mind the image of supportive therapy. Perhaps Kory needed not only to know how heartbreaking her life was but for me to hear her screams. One could say that she and Nick utilized similar defense mechanisms. Nick may also have represented a place where, for a moment, she could reach out for relationship and contact.

The dream opened up material that was painful and scary. I believed that Kory's persona of outer adaptation was coming apart. At the time, Kory did not welcome her inner agony, for she had a sense of how scary it was. She was infused with sadness. I wondered if she had felt this badly before. Given the images and feelings in this dream, I was concerned about deep, underlying suicidal tendencies. I asked her, and she said she was not suicidal, though she could not yet truly be in life either.

At the time of the dream I took note of her statement, "I am watching an anguished young man talk, but he is me." The dream in its riddle form is awakening her to let her know that she *is* this anguished young man. Jerome (the name she chose for him) is a personification of her despair. Her association that "he is like a child who was born and then his parents died" was calling attention to Kory's parental complexes, which she could no longer protect, like sacred cows, by not talking about them. Her early abandonment had had a powerful effect upon her current life. Her important relationships have been the catalyst for deep feelings of alienation.

In the session, I suggested the possibility of relating to Jerome. I sometimes ask people to name an important dream figure in order for them to feel and remember the image more fully. I had an image of Kory putting her arm around Jerome and helping him along. I felt it might be necessary for her to get to know him and embrace him in order to not become identified with him. She said that identifying with Jerome was what she was afraid of. I explained how he could have a great deal of power and that she could fall into a void with him, if she did not know about him.

Kory did not know why the name Jerome had come to her. St. Jerome was a great biblical scholar of the early church. His most important achievement was his Latin translation of the Bible. Legend tells how he removed a thorn from a lion's paw. Many paintings show Jerome in his study with the lion at his feet. To write was Kory's unlived wish. In hindsight, Kory needed this lion energy. Perhaps the lion with a thorn was a metaphor for her wounded animus. When the thorn was pulled out of the lion's paw, the animal instinct and spirit became St. Jerome's friend forever. Recently she had a dream about a lion.

I believed that Kory needed to see Jerome objectively; his pitifulness explained her tears. She had an unconscious identification with the disenfranchised Jerome, who reminded her of Jesus. I believed that she needed to integrate the lion side of her passion and rage, in other words, her own sovereignty.

At the end of the dream Kory thought someone was coming with a gun; however, it was an earthquake. A gun suggests purposefulness: it is phallic and intentional, associated with logos, rage, aggression, and sexuality. A part of her ego that came in the face of emerging phallic consciousness was threatened. Her fear of the imaginary gun may have suggested a feeling of paranoia. Perhaps both the gun and the earthquake were needed to break up her profound identification with a sadly antihero animus. The gun and earthquake frightened her to the core. I believed that movement (in the form of an "earthquake") was coming from the Self. This dream presented an unforgettable, basic psychological upheaval. The whole foundation of her life was moving.

It was three in the morning; the number three can be interpreted as signifying ego development—something was emerging into consciousness. Three is a dynamic, creative number, an intermediate number having to do with perceiving the opposites. Her mother and father left Kory when she was three. In the morning of her young life, mother earth literally moved.

The despair revealed in this dream was linked to both her mother and father. Kory's major work during the third year of analysis was focused on grieving and understanding her wound, and on how to discover her sexuality and ignite her spark—how to turn gas into fuel, into some kind of spark for her budding womanhood, her emerging feminine, sexual self.

NOTES

[1] Jung, *Symbols of Transformation, CW* 5, § 1.

[2] Toni Morrison, *Love* (New York: Knopf, 2003), p. 63.

[3] *The Golden Bough* by James George Frazer attempts to define the shared elements of religious belief. Its thesis is that old religions were fertility cults that revolved around the worship of, and periodic sacrifice of, a sacred king. "This king was the incarnation of a dying and reviving god, a solar deity who underwent a mystic marriage to a goddess of the Earth, who died at the harvest, and was reincarnated in the spring." Frazer claims that this legend is central to almost all of the world's mythologies.

[4] Samuels, *A Critical Dictionary of Jungian Analysis*, p. 32.

[5] Plato, *The Symposium*, trans. Walter Hamilton (Middlesex, England: Penguin, 1951), p. 61.

Chapter 7

Aging, Sophia, and Aphrodite's Soul

Hear me in gentleness, and learn of me in roughness.
I am she who cries out, and I am cast out on the face of the earth.
—The *Nag Hammadi Library*[1]

The little girl Snow-White grew up, and when she was seven years old, she was so beautiful that she surpassed even the queen herself. Now, when the queen asked her mirror:

Mirror, mirror, on the wall,
Who in this land is fairest of all?

The mirror said:

You, my queen, are fair; it is true.
But Little Snow-White is still
A thousand times fairer than you.

When the queen heard the mirror say this, she became pale with envy, and from that hour on, she hated Snow-White. Whenever she looked at her, she thought that Snow-White was to blame that she was no longer the most beautiful woman in the world. This twisted her heart. Her jealousy gave her no peace. Finally, she summoned a huntsman and said to him, "Take Snow-White out into the woods to a remote spot, and stab her to death. As proof that she is dead, bring her lungs and her liver back to me. I shall cook them with salt and eat them."

When Aphrodite women get old, it can be especially painful, as these women have generally not developed other sides of their personality or a wisdom that can carry them through the last half of life. After having been special for many years, wherever they go, it is painful to be unnoticed and unspecial in the eyes of the collective population. Sometimes, in their own age group, they still can retain their status. For example, my aunt Ida lives in a gated retirement community in Palm Springs, California, and is still the belle of the ball (when she is not feeling isolated and depressed).

Mirror, mirror, on the wall, who is the fairest of them all? Older Aphrodite women have great trouble with their reflection in the mirror. There is often some hope in the next botox treatment or mini-face-lift, but youth can't be bought, and often they do wish the younger ones would be killed off, like Snow-White's stepmother did.

I remember being in a trendy, Italian West Hollywood restaurant where I had gone for years, and always when I walked in, to my delight, heads would turn. Recently I visited this restaurant with my beautiful daughter, and the heads turned all right, but toward her. I thought: Yes, I have had my turn and now it is her turn. One must mature to the next stage of life or one will atrophy and not develop, and perhaps turn bitter.

For years I have read the obituaries and kept files on certain actresses and what happens to them as they age. One tragic story of a beautiful, blond Aphrodite is that of Jean Seberg, who won early fame in the title role of Otto Preminger's *Saint Joan* and went on to star in John-Luc Godard's *Breathless*. After a gossip columnist implied that Jean Seberg was pregnant by a man who was a member of the Black Panthers, she gave birth prematurely to a girl who died two days later. At the baby's funeral, a traumatized Seberg—she was thirty-one then—opened the casket to prove that the baby was white. The actress spiraled downward during the following decade. Her husband, French diplomat and novelist Romain Gary, and others close to her reported that for nine years Seberg tried to take her own life around the time of the baby's birthday. On September 8, 1979, her body was found naked in the back of a Renault parked on a Paris side street, the death credited to an overdose of barbiturates. She was from Marshalltown, Iowa. Some of the pretty girls I worked with grew up in small, Midwestern towns, and, like Seberg, suffered an even darker fate than their more hip urban sisters. In Mick Jagger's words:

> You want to get to the top of the heap from Sunset Boulevard
> Oh, it leads small-town girls astray[2]

How, then, might Aphrodite-types learn to age gracefully and wisely? In my own experience, the answer lies in depth of soul.

SOPHIA

My interest in the archetypal figure of Sophia is deeply connected with my personal search for soul. I have been identified with the energies of Aphrodite, yet it is Sophia—along with Athena—who holds my redemption, particularly as I grow older. I have suffered greatly because of my identification with Aphrodite. Throughout the course of my life I have provided a bridge to the underworld for many men, and I have been a transformative anima figure. In the *Iliad* and the *Odyssey*, both Aphrodite and Athena are the children of Zeus, with Athena as his favorite. Similarly to their father, my father was a mighty and forceful man. I know well the inflation and deflation of being both a favorite and an orphan, psychologically. I have lived out both ends of the polarity. An orphan may be described psychologically as one who has lost one or both parents. The story of the paradoxical and orphaned feminine relates strongly to my life and struggle. My father was powerful in my young eyes, as Zeus is. My mother was not a mother at all; she really barely existed. Orphanhood, abandonment, loss, and redemption have been the major themes of my life.

It is through taking on what is dark and difficult that I have developed. The alchemists sweated over their materials and themselves in their laboratories: they tortured, flayed, pounded, scored, cut, burned, and melted. Their attitude was prayerful as they tended their blessed art, the goal of which was nothing less than releasing soul from matter! In the humblest, most underrated realm, the divine soul lies ensnared and awaits its release. Perhaps in tending to this work, alchemists came into contact with what was divine in themselves.

The discovery of the figure of Sophia is not only a new and healing myth for me personally, but perhaps for our contemporary world as well. Pathology, suffering, is an intimate aspect of soul-making; it is the psyche's own method of bringing sickness and morbidity upon itself in order to change. James Hillman writes: "By Soul I mean the imaginative possibility in our natures, the experiencing through reflective speculation—dream, image, and fantasy—that mode which recognizes all realities as primarily symbolic or metaphorical."[3] We may experience soul-making through pain, through suffering depression and agony (which means "conflict," in Greek). The dark, infirm side is intrinsic to every archetype. Sickness and the disenfranchised aspects of the psyche can be a way into soul.

Knowing Sophia—Greek in name (meaning Wisdom), but evolved from multiple roots in Mesopotamia, archaic Hebrew, and the Canaanite Mother cult, as well as the Egyptian Isis tradition—has helped my Aphrodite soul. Sophia is the personified wisdom of the Universe, who achieves that wisdom through alienation and the soul's deep suffering. Sophia is a kind of living universal symbol of crushed and suffering humanity that bears within itself the undying seed of joyous resurrection. Sophia is a redeemer of the disenfranchised, the blinded, the crushed feminine. She is the universal orphan. The orphan is singular, the one and only—an individual. It is through becoming an individual, not a caricature of the ancient goddess Aphrodite, that one develops integrity.

In depth psychology, Sophia is often thought of as symbolizing the highest form of a man's anima or as representing an aspect of an actual woman who has achieved wisdom. The anima image comes in many forms, such as the myth of Sophia, the character of Sonya in Dostoevsky's *Crime and Punishment*, the sexuality of Madame Bovary, and the beauty of Helen. The anima energy is dynamic and can lead into destruction, agony, and, ultimately, soul-making. Erich Neumann writes about Sophia:

> As spirit mother she is not like the Great Mother of the lower phase, interested primarily in the infant, the child and the immature man who cling to her in these stages. She is rather a goddess of the Whole, who governs the transformation from the elementary to the spiritual level; who desires whole men knowing life in all its breadth, from elementary phase to the phase of spiritual transformation.[4]

In the Greek translation of the Hebrew scriptures (Old Testament), the name Sophia is given as a translation of the Hebrew name *Hokhmah* (meaning wisdom). Sophia is said to be the emanation of God's glory, the mirror of his energy. In Gnosticism, it is Sophia the Light that falls into the embrace of dark matter and then must be redeemed from that condition.[5] Sophia is an emblem of wisdom, morbidity, alienation, and soul. Sophia is found throughout the wisdom books of the Bible. There are many references to her in the book of Proverbs, and in the apocryphal books of Sirach and the Wisdom of Solomon. There a description of her reads: "There is in her a spirit that is intelligent, holy, unique, manifold, subtle, mobile, clear, unpolluted, distinct, invulnerable, loving the good, keen, irresistible" (Wisdom of Solomon 7:22).

In Dostoevsky's novel *Crime and Punishment,* Raskolnikov brutally murders an old crone and her sister. The act produces nightmarish guilt in Raskolnikov. He happens upon a tavern, there, he meets Marmeladov, a retired official and a drunkard. Raskolnikov learns much about the Marmeladov family, including the terrible fact that Marmeladov's daughter Sonya has had to prostitute herself in order to support the family. Marmeladov represents the grotesque sinner in Dostoevsky's display of characters. Unexpectedly, Raskolnikov is drawn into something approaching intimacy with the family. After Marmeladov, drunk as usual, falls under the horses of an approaching carriage, Raskolnikov happens to be present and takes Marmeladov home, where he dies. Raskolnikov accepts Sonia's cross, both of them begin their way of suffering and obedience. He goes and asks forgiveness from God and people at the crossroads, and then enters the police station to confess his crime. Sonia follows him to Siberia, she embodies the role of the penitent sinner who leads the way to salvation. It is only after some time in prison that his redemption and moral regeneration begin under Sonya's loving influence. He comes to the realization that happiness cannot be achieved by a reasoned plan of existence, but must be earned by suffering.

I have been particularly fascinated with the character of Sonya in *Crime and Punishment.* Sonya is the Slavonic form of Sophia. In the novel, Sonya embodies the Sophia archetype. Sonya symbolizes the passivity of the disenfranchised, the leper, the crushed feminine; she is truly the archetypal image of the sacred whore who carries wisdom and a mystical transcendence. Simmons notes that "even in that last scene in Siberia, when their intimate future together is symbolized by Raskolnikov's acceptance of their mutual lot of salvation by suffering, Sonya's role is still that of passive submission."[6] She is the universal orphan.

In the novel, when Sonya "took a step across the threshold and stood inside the room [at the home of her dying father, Marmeladov], the confession had been made and the sacrament administered." At this point in the story, Raskolnikov, who had no love in his heart and is sick and psychologically possessed, now raises the question of love, asking Poenka, Sonya's little sister, "And will you love me?" Sonya represents the transformative anima, the feminine aspect of Christ. Raskolnikov's heart is opened, and he becomes well: "I think all my illness has gone. I knew it, when I came out just now."[7] When Sonya enters, her father dies, taking the sacrament; Raskolnikov's dark spell, his possession, is dissolved. "Redemption" means to atone for, to buy back, to convert to something of value, to free from the consequences of sin, to free from bondage. Perhaps Sonya's meaning can be found in the containment, feeling, love, and loyalty she bestows on Raskolnikov, which gives him an opportunity to "buy back" his nearly hopelessly lost connection to God. Redemption occurs through his feeling experiences, which first surface when he feels compassion for Sonya's crushed and broken father, "with as much vehemence as though it were a question of his own father to carry the unconscious Marmeladov to his own room." In the epilogue, "suddenly he seemed to be seized and cast at her feet. He clasped her knees and wept." Raskolnikov was raised from the dark, cold coffin of his psyche, even as Lazarus was raised from the grave. The theme of Lazarus threads throughout the novel. Jesus raised Lazarus from the grave by saying, "Lazarus, come forth"—thus, he was one who dies twice. Toward the end of the epilogue Dostoevsky writes, "Love had raised them from the dead, and the heart of each held endless springs of life for the heart of the other."[8] The devotion of Sonya offers us a more meaningful and whole existence. She is Wisdom incarnate, the goddess of those who investigate their own psyches.

Robert Sardello notes that there is a correlation between the myth of Sophia and the soul's tasks in the coming age. He describes the images from the body of Sophia mythology as representing qualities in the material world—which, in turn, lead us to perceive everything in the material world as expressing qualities of the *interiority* of the outer world.[9] Possibly Sonya, with her "fair hair and remarkable blue eyes," is golden matter in wounded form.

Sophia is saved by her relationship with the Gnostic Jesus. Sophia, reawakened from the darkness, remembers the divine bliss of union with God, and Jesus becomes her bridegroom. Before she is saved, however, she is chained to terror, fear, grief, and abandonment. Sonya and Raskolnikov are saved by their spiritual *coniunctio* with each other; then God, the third element, enters and redemption takes place. The image and integration of Sophia can help humankind return from its slumber, transgression, and regression to a creative world.

Exploring the image of Sophia brings the *Shekhinah* to mind, the feminine image of the divine presence in the world in Jewish mystical tradition. Reports of personal experience of the Shekhinah come most frequently and dramatically when a person is suffering and weeping bitterly. The Shekhinah exists alone, in a state of alienation, cut off from home, exiled. Contemplating that state—touching that dark place in oneself where one feels orphaned, homeless, dissolute, and destitute—gives rise to her image. Yet she is also the archetype of the feminine aspect of God, his cast-off Shekhinah, buried in mire—the one who must be redeemed to bring wholeness to the cosmos.

Sophia also brings to mind Cinderella, living in the cinders of the provisional life at the borders of humanity with other cast-off creatures. Transformation is also the theme of Cinderella, a tale that holds the image of the soul suffering—in ignorance of herself and of earth, nature, and the physical body. Caitlin Matthews writes: "Cinderella is the image that has been veiled, blackened, denigrated and ignored; or else exalted, hymned and pedestalled as an allegorical abstraction of female divinity. She is allowed to be messenger, mediator, helper or handmaid."[10]

Sophia is the symbol of hope and redemption. Perhaps without her faith, one may be too sad, disenfranchised, alienated, and depressed to even wake up in the morning. Sophia's story tells us that following the path of seeking soul in the world requires us to pay attention to the "soul-spark" of that which is abandoned, thereby bringing psychological consciousness to humankind. Matthews writes:

> Sophia is the great lost Goddess. She is the Goddess of our time. By discovering her we will find our real response to the idea of divine feminine principle....The idea of Sophia is beginning to find a welcome response, the reasons not being difficult to seek. Our technological world, with its pollution and

imbalanced ecology, has brought our planet face to face with its
own mortality. Her wisdom offers a better way of life.[11]

I have contained the heritage and fate of a dual nature, of the soft
petal and hurtful thorn. The story of Sophia has opened my heart, for
it seems my fate has been to carry the opposites. I have had to carry
powerful Aphrodite energies, along with a numinous yearning to
learn—holding both amidst the shards of horrific tragedies. It is my
task to understand Sophia not just from my mind and my animus,
but from my imagination, my soul.

THE GNOSTIC SOPHIA

Ancient fourth-century papyrus manuscripts, called collectively
The Nag Hammadi Library, were discovered by an Arab peasant in
Egypt in 1945. The *Nag Hammadi Library* is a Gnostic text—the word
Gnostic refers to inner knowledge. *The Thunder, Perfect Mind* is a poetic
text from this Gnostic library—"a revelation discourse by a female
figure"—that beautifully captures the Sophia archetype in all its
stunning facets. It is as if Sophia were speaking directly to us, standing
before us in all her cosmic entirety:

> Do not be ignorant of me anywhere or any time.
> Be on your guard!
> Do not be ignorant of me.
> For I am the first and the last.
> I am the honored one and the scorned one.
> I am the whore and the holy one.
> I am the wife and the virgin.
> I am the mother and the daughter.
> I am the members of my mother.
> I am the barren one
>   and many are her sons.
> I am she whose wedding is great,
>   and I have not taken a husband.
> I am the midwife and she who does not bear.
> I am the solace of my labor pains.
> I am the bride and the bridegroom,
>   and it is my husband who begot me.
> I am the mother of my father
>   and the sister of my husband
>   and he is my offspring.[12]

ATHENA

For all of Aphrodite's compelling magnificence, if you identify only with her, then you will be limited in what you may achieve in your life. Our inner Athena is especially helpful to Aphrodite because she has so many attributes that are necessary to survive in the world—*and* she can hold her own with Aphrodite. Indeed, the fifth Homeric hymn expressly states that Aphrodite, goddess of love and beauty, cannot affect Athena, goddess of war, protectress of cities, and patroness of arts and crafts. Western philosophy had its birth in Athena's city, Athens.[15] Her most famous temple, the Parthenon, is on the Acropolis in Athens.

Ancient artists often portrayed Athena wearing a helmet and holding a magic shield. In the myth of Athena, she sprang full-grown and dressed in armor out of the forehead of Zeus, the king of the gods, who had swallowed her mother, Metis, before her birth. Athena is a child of one parent—a powerful father, to say the least—and consequently she is oriented toward the masculine. When a woman has a powerful, unusual, and creative father like Zeus, she may end up with a powerful "inner man" that can turn negative and harm tender outer relationships, particularly lovers who never match the brilliance of the father. The psychological engravings of a powerful father and lowly mother are hard to overcome, and Aphrodite's help, alone, is not sufficient. When I was young, only the stories of Aphrodite provided solace and guidance. But I also needed the "street smarts" of Athena, along with the shield of her inner perseverance and discernment. The bad or damaging father may actually be helpful to a woman in that she can no longer walk the world as an innocent, swathed only in Aphrodite's light side, but is equipped to interact with, ultimately, the dark side of the gods.

Athena is a civilized goddess (known to the Romans as Minerva), who is involved with urban matters. Athena has no consort and no offspring. The Greeks called her *Pallas*, which means maiden, or *Parthenos*, which means virgin. Her major symbol was the owl, which is sacred to the Muses and also related to prophecy and thus wisdom and the academy.[14] Athena's gray eyes bring to my mind her ability to contain—her eyes, the window to her soul, are a hue that suggests borders and liminality. She contains the opposites through soul-making and wisdom. In Homer, the color of her eyes is translated as gray-eyed, flashing-eyed, or owl-eyed.

Athena helps us with the practical realities of life: using the Internet, figuring out iPhones, thinking about politics and even entering the fray. Athena is the goddess of industry and crafts, of doing important things, not just getting men. As I have become older, it is "civilized" activities that have become increasingly meaningful to me, such as the opera, museums, architecture, and dance. Without the cultivation of Athena I do not think that I would have so great an interest in human culture, in the city, as I do now. I can imagine when I am elderly living in a city such as New York, where I could walk everywhere and fill my heart with cultural activities.

Athena is the incarnation of reason and also a warrior who defended the state against enemies coming from outside. Her tree is the olive tree. So often I have needed Athena's wisdom and energy in protecting my own boundaries from the outside as I live a complicated life in Los Angeles, yet it is the olive branch that is then needed as a symbol of peace. So often my patients are unable to say no and are eaten up by the desires of those around them; they too need her wisdom in learning to defend themselves and to activate the warrior and the peacemaker in their psyche.

Athena and Sophia are different facets of the wisdom continuum. Athena's wisdom is city-based, strategic, and involved with the outer lives of people. Sophia holds the whole, wherein the inner and outer meet. An Aphrodite woman needs both Athena and Sophia to anchor her in everyday life and in her inner life, where she draws nourishment from the whole—and not just from the gaze of a man.

I feel that my journey toward Sophia and Athena is a piece of my conversion and transformation. Perhaps wisdom will become my sister and insight my friend (Proverbs 7:4). The soul moves in the telling.

Most people enter analysis at a time of bitter weeping. They have been shaken to their core. Connection on the external or internal level has been broken—through death, loss, denial, or depression—creating a dark space that allows Sophia to enter. For that to happen, patient and analyst must take the spiritual realm seriously. Jung writes, "Whenever we speak of religious [or symbolic] contents we move in a world of images that point to something ineffable."[15] Without Sophia, the realm of the divine exists in disharmony. A daughter is missing, the feminine wanders in an alien land, and there is a persistent longing for her return.

NOTES

[1] *The Thunder, Perfect Mind*, trans. George W. MacRae and Douglas M. Parrott, in James M. Robinson, ed., *The Nag Hammadi Library*, rev. ed. (San Francisco: HarperCollins, 1978), p. 301.

[2] Mick Jagger, "Lonely at the Top," from his first solo album, *She's the Boss* (at the Live Aid, on July 13, 1985).

[3] James Hillman, *Re-Visioning Psychology* (New York: Harper & Row, 1975), p. 10.

[4] Erich Neumann, *The Great Mother* (New York: Pantheon, 1955), p. 331.

[5] Edward F. Edinger, *The Eternal Drama: The Inner Meaning of Greek Mythology* (Boston: Shambhala, 1994), p. 141.

[6] Ernest J. Simmons, "The Art of *Crime and Punishment*," in Feodor Dostoevsky, *Crime and Punishment*, (3rd edition), trans. Jesse Coulson, Georg Gibian, ed. (New York: Norton Critical Edition, 1989), p. 520.

[7] Dostoevsky, *Crime and Punishment*, trans. Jesse Coulson, pp. 157, 160-161.

[8] *Ibid.*, pp. 151, 463.

[9] Robert Sardello, "Sophia: Facing the World with Soul" (Cassette Recording, South Bend, IN: Festival of Archetypal Psychology, University of Notre Dame, 1992).

[10] Caitlin Matthews, *Sophia: Goddess of Wisdom* (Hammersmith, London: Aquarian Books, 1992), p. 5.

[11] Matthews, *Sophia: Goddess of Wisdom*, p. 8.

[12] *The Thunder, Perfect Mind*, p. 297.

[13] Edinger, *The Eternal Drama*, p. 51.

[14] Christine Downing, *The Goddess* (New York: Continuum, 1996), p. 110.

[15] C.G. Jung, *Psychology and Religion*, trans. R. F. C. Hull, Bollingen Series XX (Princeton, NJ: Princeton University Press, 1969), § 555.

Conclusion

Aphrodite's Gift

> The beginning of the *coniunctio* is set off by an ardent desire—
> Aphrodite is the mother of desires—and this desire is at the same
> time an Annunciation of the Holy Ghost.[1]
> —Edward Edinger

Edward Edinger is commenting here on the second Rosarium picture (see Chapter 5, p. 58). The dove joining the couple is significant, as was noted before: "The dove has two major symbolic references: the Holy Ghost is one, and the dove of Aphrodite is the other. So symbolically these two different aspects are put together into one paradoxical image. Now that's a union of opposites in itself. The promptings of Aphrodite and the promptings of the Holy Ghost usually aren't thought of as identical!"[2] Psychologically, that the dove descends from the star above the couple means that it is a messenger from the transpersonal or cosmic Self. This is Aphrodite's gift.

On the one hand, I have walked through my life living out the pure Aphrodite nature with which I was born—like being born tall or short, no blame—and on the other hand, the life of a Jungian analyst. Living at the Aphrodite-only level left me feeling empty and sad, but it led me to literature and then to psyche. Hillman, again: "Psyche serves in the temple of Aphrodite. Aphrodite is what makes something light up so you want it. She's the touch of beauty." I hope to be a bridge-maker to help others understand this archetype that afflicts so many women. This book is in honor of—not an attack on—Aphrodite, and points to both a love and a healthy fear of the ambivalent power of the goddess. I offer a drop of sweet dew, to help humanize the women who are afflicted by her power.

I feel modest and ambivalent about sharing these personal details of my life, and I have long pondered the appropriateness of doing so. It seems I have lived a number of lives. I still dream about being on the film set. I feel it is part of a process of redemption and possible healing to find the courage to share stories that are intimate and embarrassing to articulate. Revealing the dark and rejected treasures of one's psyche is a contribution to collective consciousness that we may all be called to make. Speaking such truths creates a point of intersection that links us together in the intimacy and community of the human psyche.

Let me conclude with the words of Jung regarding the Aphrodite-only woman:

> If a woman of this type remains unconscious of the meaning of her function, if she does not know that she is "Part of that power which would / Ever work evil but engenders good," she will herself perish by the sword she brings. But consciousness transforms her into a deliverer and redeemer.[3]

NOTES

[1] Edward F. Edinger, *The Mystery of the Coniunctio: Alchemical Image of Individuation* (Toronto: Inner City, 1994), pp. 46-47.

[2] *Ibid.*, p. 46.

[3] Jung, *The Archetypes and the Collective Unconscious*, CW 9/I, § 181.

Index

T

U

V

W

Z